D1274590

Oscar's Shadow
Wilde, Homosexuality and Modern Ireland

Oscar's Shadow
Wilde, Homosexuality and Modern Ireland

ÉIBHEAR WALSHE

CORK UNIVERSITY PRESS

First published in 2011 by
Cork University Press
Youngline Industrial Estate
Pouladuff Road, Togher
Cork, Ireland

British Library Cataloguing in Publication Data
A CIP catalogue record for this book is available from the British Library.

ISBN-978-185918-483-7
Printed in the UK by MPG Books
Typeset by Tower Books, Ballincollig, Co. Cork
www.corkuniversitypress.com

Contents

for Ciaran Wallace

Acknowledgements

In working on this study for the past ten years or so I have been aided and encouraged in so many ways and I would like to express my thanks to the following people for this support and help: David Norris, Jeff Dudgeon, Tonie Walsh, Katherine O'Donnell, Noreen Doody, Gearoid O'Brien the John Broderick archive in Athlone, Vanessa Carswell, Hugh McFadden, David Rose, Lucy McDiarmid, Caroline Williams, Terence Brown, Nicholas Grene, Alan Sinfield, Maria Pramaggorie, James H. Murphy, Joan Deane, Dermot Keogh, Pat Coughlan, Graham Allen, Alex Davis, Lee Jenkins, Mary Breen, Cliona O'Gallchoir, Heather Laird, Eamon O'Carragain, Gwenda Young, Tina O'Toole, Brian Cliff, Roy Foster, David Alderson, Joseph Bristow, Ed Madden, Sean Kennedy, Joseph Valente, Maud Ellman, Caroline Walsh, Anne Mulhall, Elizabeth Kirwan, Michael C. Cronin, Mary McAuliffe, Emma Donoghue, Edmund White, Colm Tóibín, Adrian Goodwin, Michael Waldron, Danny Pyburn, Lance Pettitt, Anne Fogarty, Derek Hand, Declan Kiberd, Chris Morash, Clair Wills, Barry Monaghan, Ken Rooney, Tina Morin, Andrew King, Alan Gibb, Ger Fitzgibbon, Pat Crowley, Siobhan Mullally, Jennifer Crowley, Elaine Hurley, Carol Quinn, Moynagh Sullivan, Sinead Gleeson, Jerusha McCormack, Eiléan Ní Chuilleanáin, Hugh McFadden, Davis Coakley and Thomas Kilroy. I would like to thank Margot Backus in particular for her generosity in reading some of these chapters and in her insightful and stimulating comments.

The project was greatly aided by a University College Cork (UCC) Arts Faculty research grant, by the support of the UCC sabbatical leave committee and of President Michael Murphy, Professor Colbert Kearney, Professor James Knowles and the UCC English Department Research committee.

The cost of the publication of this book has been helped greatly by a National University of Ireland publications grant; a UCC College of Arts, Celtic studies and Social Science publications grant; and a grant from the UCC School of English. Grateful thanks especially go to Professor Pat Coughlan for the School of English grant.

I want to thank the following scholars and institutions for invitations to lecture on Wilde and for insightful and helpful feedback: my friend

Dr Pilar Villar Argaiz, University of Granada, Spain; Juan Jose Delaney of Universidad del Salvadore, Buenos Aires, Argentina; the Abbey Theatre, Dublin; Dr Sarah McKibben at the University of Notre Dame, USA; Dr Vincent Quinn of the University of Sussex; Dr Fintan Walsh and Dr Eve Patten at Trinity College, Dublin and all at the Long Room Hub; Dr Sean Kennedy, at St Mary's College, Halifax, Canada and Professor Elizabeth Cullingford at the University of Austin at Texas.

Some of this book was completed at the Irish College in Rome in 2007 and I wish to thank the archivist, my good friend Vera Orchel, and also the vice-rector Fr Albert McDonnell and Rector Liam Bergin for their kindness and hospitality. Likewise I am very grateful to Boston College for giving me the Burns Visiting Professorship in 2006, for a very productive and pleasant time there and for all the help and support from Marjorie Howes, Liz Sullivan, Rob Savage, Vera Krielkamp, Kevin Kenny, Jim Smith, Joe Nugent and Tom Hachey.

Sections of this book have been published already: 'The Wilde Trials and Ireland', *Éire/Ireland*, Autumn 2005; 'Wilde and his Irish Biographers', *The Wildean*, No 21, July 2002; 'Wild(e) Irish', *Ireland in Proximity*, ed. Alderson (London: Routledge, 1999)

For invaluable assistance with my research I would like to thank Peggy Shannon Baker, who worked with me as a research assistant, Tomás Irish, Dr Ciaran Wallace, Dr Gerard Dineen and the librarians at the Boole Library, UCC, Trinity College, Dublin, the National Library of Ireland, the National Archives of Ireland, Burns Library, Boston College and William Clark Andrews Library, UCLA.

The text was edited with great care by Winifrid Power and Jennifer Harding. Tomás Irish very kindly helped me with the cover photograph and at Cork University Press, Maria O'Donovan and Mike Collins brought the book to print with their usual dedication and hard work. I thank them both for all the support and help. It was a pleasure working with them.

As always, I relied on my agent Jonathan Williams for his professionalism, his keen eye for copy-editing and his good humour and kindness. Special thanks on a personal level are due to Donald O'Driscoll, Celine and John Walshe, Ria White, Oonagh Cooney and Sheamus Walshe, Anne Fitzgerald, John Bergin, Michael Dillon, Jeremy Wales, Eoin Quinn, Pat Nestor, Richard Deane, Neil Ward, Rory O'Boyle, Gwenda Young, Mary Breen and Carmel Quinlan.

I would like to dedicate this book to my dear friend Dr Ciaran Wallace, for all his practical help, his encouragement and his scholarship and interest throughout the whole project. This dedication comes with my thanks and my fondest love.

PERMISSIONS:

All efforts have been made to seek permission for extracts included in this book from published and unpublished copyright works. Sincere thanks for permission given to Colm Tóibín, Jamie O'Neill, Tom Kilroy, Terry Eagleton, Michael Travers and to the Edwards mac Líammóir Literary Estate. An extract from Bernard Shaw's *My Memories of Oscar Wilde* is reproduced with permission of The Society of Authors, on behalf of the Bernard Shaw Estate. An unpublished letter from Edith Somerville is reproduced with permission of Curtis Brown Group Ltd on behalf of the estate of Edith Somerville; copyright © the estate of Edith Somerville 2011.

Preface

Oscar Wilde was the most famous gay Irishman but, as yet, no full-length book has dealt with Wilde and his homosexuality within the context of Ireland and of Irish cultural perceptions of his sexuality. This book investigates the questions: What was 'Oscar's shadow', his influence on twentieth- and twenty-first-century Irish culture and literature? What has Oscar Wilde meant to Ireland from his disgrace in May 1895 up to the present? The book begins up with what Alan Sinfield in his book *The Wilde Century* calls 'unfinished business' in Irish cultural studies – the business of a cultural history of Wilde's name, his writings and his homosexuality in modern Irish culture. The book traces Oscar's shadow in Ireland, from 1895 to the present, using contemporary Irish newspaper reports of the Wilde trials of 1895, previously unpublished archival material and a significant body of Irish critical studies, biographies and dramatisations of Wilde's life and sexuality. If perceptions of sexual identity evolve partly through public events, how then did the Irish media and literary sources configure Wilde's homosexuality during the Wilde trials and after? Wilde's homosexuality was a contested discourse within twentieth-century Ireland, a discourse that became interconnected with Irish cultural nationalism. Thus Wilde became a weathervane for the rare but contentious discussions of homosexuality in Ireland, and his life and his writings usefully intertwine within these debates. This study will set the historical context for cultural and legal perceptions of homosexuality in Ireland.

This study of the formation of homosexuality in Ireland into the twentieth century, the first such study, centres on an account of Wilde's visible presence as sexual 'other', analysing the strategies of normalisation used to police his unnameable sin within Irish media and literary accounts. The book argues that Wilde in Irish culture was perceived not so much as Oscar Wilde the unspeakable but much more as Oscar Wilde the dissident Irishman. Wilde, famous for his writings and notorious for his sexuality, is central for perceptions of homosexuality in modern Ireland.

Éibhear Walshe, School of English.
University College Cork, Ireland, 2011

1. Ireland and
the Wilde trials:
1884–1907

To be sure, sexuality is not a fixed entity, either in an individual or in a culture. Nonetheless, a postmodern idea of Wilde (and everything else) as endlessly elusive can obscure the real determinants in cultural change. Twentieth-century uses of Wilde's name, certainly, have depended on simplifications, mistaken apprehensions and downright falsehoods. However, the point is not Wilde's true identity, but the identity that the trials foisted on him. It was not who he was, but who we have made him to be. I want to suggest that there is unfinished business here; that Ireland, as much as England and the United States, might claim the name of Wilde as a gay icon. (Alan Sinfield, '"I See It Is My *Name* that Terrifies": Wilde in the Twentieth Century'[1])

What did Ireland make of its most famous gay son, Oscar Wilde? In his book *The Wilde Century*,[2] Alan Sinfield has argued persuasively that the name, fate and public persona of Wilde formed the central twentieth-century cultural concept of the 'homosexual' in Britain. This book examines the representations of the figure of Oscar Wilde, his life, his writings and his sexuality in twentieth-century Irish cultural discourse. How did Irish writers, newspapers, critics and biographers view his homosexuality in relation to his Irishness? Like Sinfield, my interest is with some 'unfinished business' in Irish cultural studies: an examination of how Wilde's name and his 'crime' provoked public discussion about homosexuality in modern Irish culture.

Ireland was undergoing a period of radical self-fashioning in the years after Wilde's disgrace, particularly in the years before political independence in 1922, and therefore attitudes towards his name and his sexuality became implicated in this time of flux, this cultural volatility. Furthermore, Wilde's own writings and his interconnected public persona were much more complex than any of his Irish contemporaries because of the ambivalent strategies of self-representation he deployed to mask his homosexuality. Wilde's writings create a kind of imaginative mutability, both hinting at and then containing his sexuality.[3] Maria Luddy argues that 'The late nineteenth and early twentieth century in Ireland was a period of great upheaval. In time of upheaval, issues about sexual morality often become a focus of attention and anxiety.'[4] Wilde,

1

more than any other Irish writer, became the focus for such attention and anxiety.

Irish reactions to Wilde's sexuality since his trials and imprisonment in 1895 have varied widely but rarely have been informed by the voracious homophobia of British public discourse. To give an example of that variety, perhaps the sole hostile account of Wilde came from the Belfast playwright St John Ervine, who wrote in his book *Oscar Wilde: A Present Time Appraisal*:

> There is, perhaps, too much tendency today to make light of sodomy, too great a tendency to condemn harshly without attempting to understand those who were most ferocious in their denunciation of Wilde's offences. Neither of the Wildes had any sanctity to dispense. Their second son Oscar was damned on the day that he was born and would have done better to have died in childhood as his sister Isola, who followed him, did.[5]

In contrast, other Irish sources can be surprisingly sympathetic towards Wilde and his sexual 'sin'. Witness this account from Lucy McDiarmid's *The Irish Art of Controversy* of an exchange of letters to *The Irish Times* in 1973 on the subject of homosexuality, provoked by Roger Casement's earlier reburial in Glasnevin cemetery in Dublin (as I will discuss later, Casement is a revealing counterpoint to Wilde, a figure always at the centre of Irish controversy and debate, while Wilde was often invisible):

> Here and there in exchanges unrecorded in the papers, a hidden Ireland persisted, tolerant of sexual preferences. . . . Mrs Ita Kelly of Ballsbridge wrote in to 'concur' with a previous letter writer, Mrs Irving, who had claimed that homosexuality was 'just another kind of loving'. To this opinion, Mrs Kelly added an anecdote from her school days 'many moons ago' under the tutelage of Mother Scholasticia. Reading *The Ballad of Reading Gaol* to her students, Mother Scholasticia explained that Wilde had been imprisoned 'just for loving another man'. Mrs Kelly called this a 'splendid reply to a class of girls of seventeen years old' and wished Mother Scholasticia were alive to participate in the present correspondence: 'Her opinions certainly would be very valuable.' The obscure but radical Mother Scholasticia was, said her student, a brilliant intellectual 'whose authority the girls never questioned'.[6]

My argument is that, despite some moments of homophobia, Irish sources accommodate the 'sinner' Wilde within some aspects of nationalist discourse. At the historical moment in European culture when the idea of the homosexual as a dangerous type was evolving, Irish nationalist discourses were deployed in some areas of cultural life to rescue or absolve Wilde from this aberrant sexual identity.

In this chapter, I want to trace the process by which Oscar Wilde could be commandeered into the acceptable mode of the Irish rebel in the aftermath of his public disgrace. If perceptions of sexual identity evolve partly through public events, then how did the Irish media and literary sources attempt to configure Wilde's homosexuality during the 1895 trials and after? As Sinfield suggests, the question is not simply about who Wilde actually was, either sexually or racially, but about what we make him stand for. Here, I chart the revealing ways in which Wilde's homosexuality became a contested discourse in Ireland during his Old Bailey trials of 1895, a discourse that became implicated with that of Irish cultural nationalism. My argument is that there was a surprisingly reticent, even tolerant, attitude evident towards Wilde in many of the mainstream Irish newspapers, and this reticence stands in marked contrast to the energetic homophobia of the English newspapers. It also contrasts with the Irish media coverage of two other homosexual scandals in Dublin: the 1884 Dublin Castle scandal and the 1907 stealing of the Irish Crown jewels, where opportunistic nationalist anger against Crown administrators was expressed in virulently homophobic newspaper outpourings.

Wilde's three trials of 1895 took place at a crucial juncture in the making of the modern idea of the homosexual. Michel Foucault has argued that only in the nineteenth century did the homosexual become a type or a personage with a past and a case history. In Ireland, as in other societies towards the end of the nineteenth century, modern ideas of sexual identity began to take shape and draw meaning from visible mainstream cultural events. Jeffrey Weeks writes:

> Homosexuality moved from being a category of sin to become a psychological disposition . . . but the idea that there is such a thing as *the* homosexual person is a relatively new one. All the evidence suggests that before the eighteenth century homosexuality, interpreted in its broadest sense as involving erotic activities between people of the same gender, certainly existed, 'homosexuals' did not.[7]

In Ireland, same-sex activity between men had been criminalised since Henry VIII assumed control of the monasteries in 1536 and seized control of the prerogatives of the ecclesiastical courts, making sodomy a crime. Homosexuality had been a sin and was now a crime, but would not become a sexual identity until the second half of the nineteenth century.

Interestingly enough, some of the most infamous cases of trials for sodomy were amongst the Anglo-Irish and sometimes from within Wilde's own Irish Protestant class. For example, Mervyn Touchet, Earl of Castlehaven, was tried in the House of Lords in 1631 for sodomy and adultery, and executed on 14 May 1631. In 1640, John Atherton, Lord Bishop of Waterford and Lismore, was hanged in Dublin for sodomy. In a later famous case in 1822, Percy Jocelyn, Bishop of Clogher, was found *in flagrante delicto* with a soldier, but broke bail and fled to Scotland where he died in disgrace. Each of these cases represented individual acts of sexual disgrace, rather than any cumulative sense of a knowable homosexual identity, and it was only with Wilde that the conjunction of private sexual acts and public exposure marked a sustained engagement with the idea of the Irish homosexual as an identifiable type.

Wilde's trials took place during a crucial period of definition for the idea of an urban homosexual identity, as much in Ireland as in Britain and elsewhere. Matt Holbrook, writing about London from 1885 to the outbreak of the First World War in 1914 suggests that:

> These years were marked by burgeoning debate and concern about homosexuality and came towards the end of a half century of massive upheaval in the rapidly expanding British capital. Following Michel Foucault and Jeffrey Weeks's pioneering work in the 1970s, literary and lesbian and gay scholars have variously examined the significance of the law, newspapers, sexology, aestheticism and decadence and Hellenism to shifting ideas of homosexuality during the period of discussion here. This field of debate and writing provided distinctive frames of reference through which homosexual relations were experienced, condemned and celebrated.[8]

Much has been written on British media treatments of the Wilde trials, but little or nothing on the Irish sources. The local newspaper coverage of the trials drew out an ambivalent and often contradictory contestation about Wilde's sexual sin from within Irish cultural discourse. The Irish newspapers struck a markedly differing note from their British counterparts, and subsequent writers from Ireland, notably Shaw, Yeats, Joyce and Behan, 'nationalised' Wilde (a word I borrow from Margot Norris) by claiming him as a figure of affirming dissidence.[9] In this national appropriation of Wilde, these later artists could reconfigure his unsettling sexual sin by seeing it as the causal factor within an episode of anti-imperialist defiance. My argument is that some subsequent Irish writers, particularly Anglo-Irish, saw Wilde as a disruptive figure of anti-colonial resistance, and this reconstruction, in some ways, mitigated his aberrant homosexuality for those writers and indeed for their society. The powerfully homophobic culture of twentieth-century Ireland invented strategies by which the 'unspeakable' Oscar could be reclaimed as Wilde the Irish rebel.

Ambiguities abound in Wilde's life and work, not least in his own representations of himself as a sexual being. Nevertheless, the useful and incontestable fact remains that, in May 1895, an Irishman named himself publicly as a lover of other men, although qualifying this declaration of homosexual identity by falsely claiming that his love for other men had never been expressed sexually. At a critical moment in his trial, Wilde defined 'the love that dare not speak its name' by citing a proud genealogy of same-sex lovers. The significance of Wilde's speech, in this context, is that for the first time we have an Irishman making a public affirmation of homosexual love. However, this was not the first public debate about Irishness and homosexuality in the latter half of the nineteenth century.

More than ten years earlier, another court case in Dublin also dealt with this forbidden topic, the so-called Dublin Castle scandal of 1884. Public discussion about homosexuality was very different in this case and so it is illuminating to contrast Irish newspaper coverage of the earlier scandal with that of the Wilde trials. In May 1884, the Irish nationalist politician William O'Brien publicly alleged that there had been same-sex activities involving Dublin Castle administrators. In his newspaper *United Ireland*, O'Brien's allegations gave voice to what H. Montgomery Hyde describes as 'the widespread belief that homosexual "vice" was rampant in official circles in Ireland'.[10] According to historian Leon O'Broin:

> Ugly reports had been in circulation for some time about the sexual perversions of some of the headquarter officers in Dublin Castle. The Nationalist members of parliament attacked Spencer and Trevelyan [Dublin Castle administrators] and imputed them with the misdeeds of their employees. Tim Healy [Nationalist politician] with typical sarcasm, alleged that Spencer's services to the state had well entitled him to promotion and suggested that he should become the duke of Sodom and Gomorrah.[11]

The rumours and indirect reporting came to a head when, in a libel case that would be repeated during the Wilde trials, O'Brien used his newspaper to make allegations, particularly about Gustavus Cornwall, the secretary of the General Post Office in Dublin. As with Wilde's action against the Marquis of Queensberry, Cornwall sued O'Brien for libel. The trial opened on 2 July 1884. Extensive police evidence of same-sex activities was brought against Cornwall and others; not only was O'Brien cleared of libel, but Cornwall and seven other men, including a shopkeeper from Rathmines in Dublin, James Pillar, were now under police surveillance. Subsequently, they were all arrested and tried on 5 August 1884 in Green Street Court House in Dublin on charges relating to indecency and sodomy. In July 1884, the Crown prosecution took witness statements from many of the men charged at Inn's Quay police station, in particular against James Pillar, and these police records survive. These sworn statements provide rare historical evidence of homosexual social networks in the Dublin of the 1880s. This was a time when, as Matt Cook has written of London, 'homosexuality was woven into the fabric of urban culture'.[12]

James Pillar's shop was clearly a meeting place for men of all ages in Dublin and it was alleged that he kept a room behind his shop specifically for parties and assignations, nicknamed 'Eveline's Bower'. These witness depositions, from men like Malcolm Johnston, a man of independent means, a Corporal George Sinclair of the Scots Fusiliers and Private Allen of the Highland Light Infantry, reveal widespread casual male prostitution amongst British soldiers in Dublin. Apart from paid homosexual activity, there was also clearly a network of homosexual men who wanted to have sex with other men, freely and without pay, like 26-year-old Peter Behan, a dairyman, known as Topsy Keogh, who had been sexually active from the age of fourteen. There was a highly developed language of camp nicknames and slang between all the men who moved within this subculture. George Taylor, an employee of the British and Irish Steam Packet Company, was known as the 'Maid of Athens' and a Lieutenant Sankey was known as 'Baby', and these witness statements reveal a community, a language and an urban identity all centred on same-sex activities in the Dublin of the 1880s. (There were even references made by one witness statement to a 'bitches ball', a ball for male prostitutes.) A letter written from London in December 1883 by Malcolm Johnston, known as 'Lady Constance Clyde', to James Pillar, called 'Pa', was copied into the witness statements and survives in full, the only surviving evidence of a self-consciously camp Irish gay subculture at the end of the nineteenth century.

> My Dear Pa,
>
> Many thanks for all your sweet notes. I have been in the hands of the police (don't be frightened) or rather the other way, the police have been in my hands so many times lately that my lily white hands have been trembling and I am utterly fucked out. Such camp. I had my first L.G. from Windsor seeing me yesterday in plain clothes, such a beauty!! Nearly all the police about here have been up in the evenings, having a 'drop of the crature', some I have done, others I only kissed, a kissing one was up last night, and a fucking one two nights previous. Some of the titled ladies (damnable bitches) looked up amongst the peerages and discovered to my agony that such a title as Lady Constance Clyde existed not, consequently my title was taken from me and I am forced to acknowledge, now, that I have been discovered assuming a false name, that I never was Lady, but plain Miss Phoenix Park. Such vicissitudes of fortune to be sure !!! . . . I am so

glad Miss Cregan was pleased with the gown I gave her, now is her time to make her fortune before she wears it out or gets white sauce (oysters I mean) on it. I really must conclude and I assure you, you have all the best wishes for a prosperous and happy new year from

Ever Yours Truly
Phoenix Park[13]

During this second trial, other gay men were called as witnesses against Cornwall, but, because they were in danger of losing their own jobs, they were reluctant to give evidence against him. In his memoirs, the profoundly homophobic O'Brien characterises this reluctance as 'one of those sudden gusts of infantile fretfulness which is apt to sweep over persons of their peculiar mentality . . . [when] the three essential witnesses refused to be examined'.[14] 'Providentially', he further observed, 'the cowardice of persons thus diseased is commonly as abject as their depravity.'[15]

By the end of 1884, the trials finally concluded and a number of the men were found guilty and sentenced to hard labour. James Pillar was sentenced to twenty years' penal servitude. However, the central protagonist, Cornwall, was acquitted and, due to retire anyway, he resigned from his post in Dublin Castle. According to O'Broin, however, 'Cornwall lost his post office job for having, as a Dublin wag put it, tampered with Her Majesty's males.'[16]

Most noteworthy is the fact that publicity around the Dublin Castle trials provoked widespread Irish newspaper condemnation of homosexuality. All Irish papers distanced themselves from what they chose to see as a foreign vice, attacking for purposes of nationalist rhetoric. In the *United Ireland* of 7 June 1884, O'Brien wrote of the defendants' homosexuality as 'the system of depravity unsurpassed in the history of human crime' and compared it with 'the comparatively venial crimes (as far as human society is concerned) of the Moonlighters and Invincibles'.[17] Other accounts stressed the un-Irishness of those accused: the *Evening Telegraph* attacked Cornwall for 'contaminating the running stream of Irish moral purity by stirring up the sink of pollution implanted by foreign hands in its very edges',[18] while the *Dundalk Democrat* noted sodomy as 'a crime that was unmentionable and happily is unknown and was previously unheard of by ninety-nine out of every hundred of the people in this country'.[19]

In the light of Irish media accounts of the Dublin Castle scandal, the coverage of Wilde's arrest and trial is striking. Irish newspapers, again obliged to confront the dangerous topic of homosexuality, side-stepped the issue by concentrating on Irish nationalist outrage at British legal injustice. By 1895, now that an Irishman was at the centre of the scandal and not a collection of hated Dublin Castle administrators, the discourse about homosexuality became much less direct, more circumspect, than that appearing in the English press.

Linked to this circumspection in the Irish newspapers at the time was a tendency within later Irish sources to interpret Wilde's behaviour in the courtroom of the Old Bailey as heroic and politicised. In other words, Wilde's defence against the charge of homosexuality and gross indecency was later claimed for the tradition of Irish Republican defiance in the face of British injustice. In particular, when, during the trial, Wilde was asked to define the exact nature of 'the love that dare not speak its name', a line from a coded poem about homosexuality by Lord Alfred 'Bosie' Douglas, his response would be seen as one of the great Irish anti-imperialist speeches from the dock. Seamus Heaney asserted a full century after Wilde's ordeal that 'during his trials in 1895, Wilde had been magnificent in the dock and had conducted himself with as much dramatic style as any Irish patriot ever did'.[20]

Wilde wasn't exactly being truthful and certainly not being patriotic when he denied the sexual element in the love that dare not speak its name, but his declaration broke the wall of public silence about homosexuality when he brought it to a point of public utterance.[21] His homosexual love did have to speak its name when the law demanded an answer, however partial that answer would be. The simple fact that he made such a profession of ennobling same-sex love is in itself precisely the factor that provoked public disturbance and debate. The vital importance here is Wilde's articulation of the homoerotic; important, that is, for Irish public discourse. Martyrs and figures of political rebellion are often constructed retrospectively and this was the case with Wilde in Ireland. Shaw, Yeats and others would interpret Wilde's downfall in the light of the literary and political career of his mother, Speranza, a view aligning him with the rhetorical traditions of nineteenth-century Protestant Irish Republicanism and, indirectly, with the many impassioned speeches made by Irish activists in English courtrooms during the nineteenth century. As I shall suggest, these later readings of Wilde the Irish rebel served to mitigate the potential severity of Irish commentators, in particular in dealing with his sexuality, and thus are linked to the Irish newspapers' discretion when reporting directly on his trials.

The three trials of Oscar Wilde in 1895 and the consequent newspaper coverage provide us with a moment of crucial engagement with the question of homosexuality in Ireland. Linda Dowling argues that Wilde's statement in the trial created 'a new language of moral legitimacy, pointing forward to Anglo-American decriminalisation and, ultimately, a fully developed assertion of homosexual rights.'[22] But did his statement create a language of moral legitimacy for homosexual rights in Ireland? Certainly his disgrace radicalised Wilde's own sense of his sexuality after his release and subsequent exile in continental Europe. He wrote to his friend and first lover, Robert Ross, in February 1898, making an implicit link between patriotism and Uranian love:

> A patriot put in prison for loving his country loves his country, and a poet in prison for loving boys loves boys. To have altered my life would have been to have admitted that Uranian love is ignoble. I hold it to be noble – nobler than other forms.[23]

From the trials onwards, Wilde's name and his fate elicited very particular perceptions and notions of homosexuality. In Britain, as Ed Cohen and Michael Foldy have shown, the Wilde trials had the effect of drawing out homophobia from the British press.[24] Because of the unmentionable nature of his sexual sin, Wilde's body became the site for displaced unease. For Cohen:

> It is hardly surprising that the newspaper reporting of Wilde's prosecution conjoined the spectacular and the characterlogical in order to figure 'Oscar Wilde' as embodying a new type of sexual offender. As soon as Wilde himself became the subject of legal scrutiny, it was very clear that it was his body that was at stake in the production of public meaning engendered by the case.[25]

In the Irish newspapers these same issues of unease and sexual phobia are evident as Wilde's body featured as a site for contested meaning, a means by which his sexuality could be indirectly named. But in Ireland this unease becomes ambivalent, undermined by Irish public resentment of British imperialism.

Until 1895, his Irishness empowered Wilde as a writer of comedies of manners. Declan Kiberd notes that the 'ease with which Wilde effected the transition from stage Ireland to stage England was his ultimate comment on the shallowness of such categories . . . To his mortification and intermittent delight, Wilde found that his English mask was not, by any means, a perfect fit.'[26] However, from the outset of the first trial, Wilde's celebrity was transformed into notoriety by Queensberry's accusation that he was posing as a 'somdomite' [sic]. Wilde himself had written in *The Soul of Man under Socialism* of 'that monstrous and ignorant thing that is called Public opinion'.[27] Now, this monstrous and ignorant thing moved against Wilde to demonise him as a corrupter of youth and a destroyer of innocence. Foldy shows that 'the Wilde Trials were unusual in that they provided a single forum and a single frame of reference for all of these otherwise disparate concepts: "decadence", "degeneracy" and "same sex passion"'.[28] Xenophobia, as well as homophobia, prompted attacks on

Wilde's decadent foreignness, but it was the idea of his 'French' decadence rather than his Irish unruliness which fuelled the public attacks in
Britain. Foldy points out that Wilde:

> represented a frightening constellation of threats which conflated all
> these disparate elements and associations: he represented foreign
> vice, foreign art and indirectly, the legacy of foreign rulers . . . thus
> when the newspapers attacked Wilde and condemned his foreign
> vice, they were also expressing their xenophobic fear of foreigners and
> foreign influences, their hatred of a useless and parasitic aristocracy,
> and their intolerance for useless artists and for anyone who would
> actively try to subvert the status quo.[29]

Wilde's own foreignness as an Irishman was evidently little used by the
English newspapers as a weapon to attack his sexual otherness, and only
at a late stage of the trials, when conviction seemed imminent, was his
Irishness directly referred to in court.[30] At the end of the third trial, Sir
Edward Clarke, the defence lawyer, urged the jury to acquit Wilde, using
the following mitigating plea of his racial otherness (Clarke apparently
felt that he had no other extenuating plea to offer):

> If upon an examination of the evidence you therefore feel it your duty
> to say that the charges against the prisoner have not been proved, then
> I am sure that you will be glad that the brilliant promise which has
> been clouded by these accusations, and the bright reputation which
> was so early clouded in the torrent of prejudice which a few weeks ago
> was sweeping through the press, have been saved by your verdict from
> absolute ruin: and thus it leaves him, a distinguished man of letters
> and a brilliant Irishman, to live among us a life of honour and repute
> and to give in the maturity of his genius gifts to our literature of which
> he has given only the promise of his early youth.[31]

Noreen Doody comments that Clarke perhaps appealed 'to the generally accepted nineteenth-century view of the Irish as less responsible
than their English "betters"'.[32] This late reference to the defendant's
racial identity, however, proved futile, and Clarke failed to develop it
further, but subsequent Irish accounts of the trials and of the convicted
man's decision to face arrest afterwards seized upon Wilde's national
pride and sense of honour as motivating his behaviour. Irish sources
came to lionise Wilde for his racial difference, his Anglo-Irish pride and
old-fashioned chivalry.

Since Wilde's third trial, in May 1895, dealt most directly with his
homosexuality, the coverage of that trial in a range of Irish newspapers is
illuminating. Major Irish newspapers like *The Irish Times* carried daily
accounts, but most of these reports were discreet and impersonal.

(Exceptions were accounts in the *Irish News* and *Belfast Morning News* on 27 May 1895 informing readers that 'Oscar Wilde, who lived on an extraordinary reputation, has thus disappeared and let us hope the last has been heard of him'.) Irish newspapers were reticent in reporting court proceedings and were reluctant also to name the defendant's crime. As Cohen and Foldy have demonstrated, the British press also avoided direct mention of same-sex activities by displacing that unnameable sin on to Wilde's body. The Irish press, however, maintained a distance from Wilde's sin and from his body: on 24 May the *Evening Herald* even ran its coverage of the trials under the heading 'Wilde's defence: Accused extremely unwell and talked with concern about his anxiety'.

The Irish Times carried two brief paragraphs, while the *Cork Examiner* published short daily notices concerning the trial between 22 and 27 May 1895. But *The Irish Times* paid much more attention to the parallel story of the public fist fight between the Marquis of Queensberry and his son Lord Douglas of Hawick, a fracas that took place in the course of the trial, as did the *Cork Constitution*, which had some fun poking comedy out of this messy dispute within the Douglas family. On 22 May, the *Cork Examiner* made its first reference to the trial by discussing the 'specific charges' concerning Wilde's co-accused, Alfred Taylor: but these charges are unnamed, as is Wilde. More is made of the fight between Queensberry and his son, presumably a safer topic in the reporting on 24 May and on 25 May; however, the paper does finally mention Wilde as 'betraying tokens of the keenest anxiety' on 25 May. Only on 27 May, when Wilde had been sentenced, did the *Cork Examiner* refer directly to 'immoral practices', but with a great deal of sympathy for the 'ill and anxious' defendant. The *Clare Journal* likewise carried a very business-like account of Wilde's conviction, without any comment beyond the bare facts, on 27 May, but did raise the question of Lord Alfred Douglas's absence from the court and the possibility of his being arrested. The *Irish Catholic* said nothing at all about Wilde and the trials, even though it paid great attention to the career of William O'Brien. The *Galway Vindicator* also kept a silence on the Wilde trials, apart from a short notice on 8 May about the attendance of Wilde's solicitors in chambers. However, the *Galway Vindicator* (5 June) did carry in full a letter from the London newspapers under the subheading 'Oscar Wilde's clerical bailsman'. This letter was Stewart Hedlam's justification for standing bail for Wilde, published in the *Church Recorder*.

> I think it is due to my friends to make the following statement. I became bail for Mr Oscar Wilde on public grounds. I felt that the actions of a large section of the Press, of the theatrical managers at whose houses his plays were running and of his publishers, were

calculated to prejudice his case before the trial had even begun. I was
a surety not for his character but for his appearance in court to attend
his trial. I had very little personal knowledge of him at the time. I think
I had only met him twice but my confidence in his honour is fully justified by the fact that (if rumour be correct, withstanding strong
inducements to the contrary) he stayed in England and faced his trial.
Now that the trial is over and Mr Wilde has been convicted and sentenced I still feel that I was absolutely right in the course I took and I
hope that when he has gone through his sentence, Mr Wilde may be
able with the aid of his friends to do good work in his fresh life.[33]

The *Belfast Newsletter* used the words 'gross indecency' about Taylor
on 22 May and the next day gave details of the rent-boy evidence. But
when finally, on 27 May, the newspaper devoted a full-length article to
the case, it confined itself to writing about 'certain misdemeanours' and
'improper motives'. This reticence appeared when the English newspapers were far harder on Wilde. Against this, consider this from the
'London Letter' of the *Cork Constitution* on 27 May 1895, just after
Wilde had been sentenced:

> All who heard the trial of Wilde and Taylor say the sentence passed
> upon the prisoners is not a whit too severe. These persons – I shall not
> call them privileged – describe the evidence as revolting. The sen-
> tence, as a matter of fact, is the most severe known to the law. It is not
> confinement only that indeed might be borne with equanimity. It is
> the complemental [*sic*] infliction of hard labour that the sting, the
> misery, the degradation exists. The interpretation of the term in prison
> covers all that is demoralising and crushing. The maximum of loath-
> some and humiliating labour has to be borne by a system reduced
> through the thinnest and most rigid dietary to a point just above actual
> collapse. Such a life, even for two brief years, to a man of luxurious
> habits crowds by a refinement of skilful pressure all that is conceivable
> in exacting toil and shameful degradation supplemented by associ-
> ating with the scum of the earth, quite ready themselves to heap upon
> this particular criminal the unspeakable loathing aroused by his
> offence. A leper would not exchange places with Wilde.[34]

Why was the Irish press so discreet in the coverage of the Wilde trials?
Several factors may have accounted for such discretion, one being the
Republican legacy of his mother. More crucially, the political climate in
Dublin – with the growing pressure in southern Ireland for political
autonomy – may well have muted any condemnation of an Irishman at
odds with the British legal and political establishment. In the earlier
Dublin Castle scandal of 1884, the investigation reflected not just homo-
phobic unease with same-sex activities, but the antipathy Irish nationalist

politicians felt towards colonial administrators. Although Wilde's nationality failed to protect him during his trials in London, it may have provided him with some mitigating cover within Irish society at a time of rising nationalism.

In contrast to the reticence of other Irish newspapers, however, the *Freeman's Journal* of 27 May 1895 carried an unusually lengthy discussion of Wilde's conviction; but even at this very early stage, the Irish commentator clearly found himself in a tricky, often contradictory, position. The anonymous journalist, 'our own correspondent', devotes a substantial portion of his general report on London affairs to condemning Wilde. His discussion of the case and the sentencing follows the usual pattern of condemnation: he makes no direct mention of Wilde's homosexuality, but, instead, the defendant's body becomes the site upon which the trial's sexual significance can be inscribed. In Cohen's words, Oscar Wilde's body is now 'a descriptive trope that personalises the criminal proceedings'.[35] On 27 May 1895 the *Freeman's Journal* correspondent employs terms familiar in the London press such as 'horrid', 'festering corruption' and 'abominations' to justify the sentence:

> As to the horrid character of Wilde's crime, it is quite superfluous to add anything to what Judge Wills, who held the scales of justice with scrupulous fairness, said in passing sentence. The remarkable thing is to discover now that Oscar Wilde was at the centre of festering corruption seems to have been known in the artistic and theatrical circles in which he moved. But it is satisfactory anyway to feel that even the most brazen effrontery in the pursuit of such abominations does not bring immunity from punishment. It is even said that the police could lay their hands on fifty men well known in society who are equally guilty with him and whose connection with this odious scandal has been notorious for years.[36]

The correspondent's view of a queer community hidden within artistic and theatrical circles – of a covert secret society, with Wilde at the centre – shifts the perception of homosexuality from individual acts of sexual activity towards the notion, albeit hostile, of a community created out of sexual preference. The analysis then moves from a general denunciation of the defendant's culpability and incorporates two accounts of his public appearances in 1895, one just before the trials, on stage at the first night of *An Ideal Husband* in March, and the other at the end of the trials in the dock of the Old Bailey. Here, descriptions of Wilde's body, his dress and his demeanour are encoded through the interpolation of terms such as 'condescending' and 'insolence', within the rhetoric of sexual decadence and arrogance; such writing provides the evidence that the defendant was indeed 'a centre of festering corruption' and focuses public attention on his body. As Cohen notes, 'the press corps anticipated the legal attachment of Wilde's body by confining/defining him within their interpretative gaze'.[37]

> Some months ago I saw Oscar Wilde at the first night of 'An Ideal Husband'. He was then in the zenith of his fame . . . Wilde himself was in a stage box, being flattered and lionized by a party of most distinguished persons – men and women whose praise he condescendingly accepted. He was dressed in a last note of fashion, faultlessly groomed and assuming airs of semi-royal graciousness to an admiring audience. He strutted in from the wings with an air of contemptuous indifference, one hand in his trouser pocket, and an opera hat in his other . . . The object of this ovation responded with a shrug of the shoulders suggesting a feeling of deprecatory boredom. When silence had been restored, he drawled out a few words of studied insolence and retired.[38]

Then Wilde's body is reconstructed as in an 'outing', a public exposure of his hidden sexuality. With puritanical glee, the writer contrasts Wilde's bodily frailty and obvious physical strain with his earlier physical arrogance.

> I saw Oscar Wilde on Friday last in the dock of the Old Bailey and a more shocking contrast could not possibly be conceived. The aspect of sleek, well-fed luxuriousness had vanished, the cheeks were lined and flabby, and wore a most unearthly colour. His eyes were bloodshot and expressive of the last stage of acute terror, the eyes of a man who might at any time get a fatal seizure from overstrain. His hair was all in disorder and he crouched into a corner of the dock with his face turned towards the jury and the witness box, his head resting on his hand so that it was almost hid from the public . . . The general impression he conveyed was of a man filled with a vague hopeless terror, not of one filled with shame at the dreadful ignominy of his position.[39]

In this shifting representation of Wilde's physicality, which renders him bestial and inhuman, the body becomes the site for displaced horror at an unnamed sexual sin. No longer the arrogant playwright strutting on to the stage, the terrorised defendant now attempted to hide his body from the public gaze, even though he lacked the appropriate shame and penitence before his sexual sin. Up to this passage, the *Freeman's Journal* account follows patterns of representation and condemnation appearing in English versions of the trials. However, as he discusses the judicial proceedings, 'our own [Irish] correspondent' raises issues absent from English coverage. Reminding his readers that the jury in the second trial was dismissed because of its failure to reach a unanimous verdict of guilty

for Wilde, he recalls that the abrupt ending of that trial led to press speculation that the jury might themselves have been 'corrupt' or biased in
Wilde's favour, thus sexually suspect. 'Our own correspondent' then
reveals his national identity and his nationalist fervour:

> We all know what trial by jury is – in England. It is the palladium of
> English justice and all the rest of it. It is a peculiarly English institu-
> tion which the 'Celtic Fringe' is quite incapable of appreciating or
> utilising at its proper value . . . Mere Irish juries had been accused
> freely in agrarian or political cases of refusing to place absolute trust
> in the evidence of policemen or informers but here was a London
> jury without the suspicion of an Irishman about it accused of being
> actuated by what among the 'Celtic Fringe' would be regarded as an
> immeasurably baser motive in refusing to find the prisoners guilty . . .
> It is impossible to escape the conclusion that an Old Bailey jury must
> be very amenable to influences of this kind and that the high-flown
> eulogies we have been accustomed to from English orators in the
> House of Commons on the immaculate character of the English
> juries as compared with Irish are mere pharisaical humbug.[40]

Cohen argues that Wilde's identification as a homosexual was produced in reaction to its opposite, the heterosexual: for an identity to take
shape, it needed its binary opposite. However, in the terms of Irish cultural discourse, Wilde, as sexual 'other', was made safe within another
discourse of oppositional types, that of Celtic versus British. The sexual
'type' of homosexuality, invoking Wilde's guilt and 'festering corruption',
is collapsed into an anti-imperialist discourse; thus, as the writer moves
into a lengthy diatribe against British justice, we lose sight of Wilde's
contaminated body.

This contemporary Irish account in the *Freeman's Journal* is probably
the first to subsume Wilde's homosexuality into the national question. If
we consider the next homosexual scandal to take place in pre-indepen-
dence Ireland, the so-called Irish Crown jewels theft of July 1907, again
nationalist Ireland could be homophobic if the sexual scandal involved
Crown officials. When King Edward VII and Queen Alexandra visited
Dublin that summer, in the words of Hyde, 'Dublin Castle was the
scene of another scandal with homosexual undertones'.[41] Just before the
royal party reached Dublin, the Insignia of the Order of St Patrick, the
so-called Irish Crown jewels, were stolen from a safe in Dublin Castle.
The theft was discovered on 6 July and, as Montgomery Hyde writes, 'the
officer responsible for their safe keeping was the Ulster King of Arms, Sir
Arthur Vicars, and a homosexual aged forty-three. Sir Arthur shared a
house with his assistant, the Athlone Pursuivant, Francis Shackleton,
also homosexual'.[42]

A royal commission was set up to investigate, but King Edward VII intervened to adjourn the commission after only a week of hearings, alarmed because, in Myles Dungan's account of the affair, there was 'evidence of the existence of a group of homosexuals associated with the Office of Arms'.[43] This group of homosexuals was rumoured to include Vicars, Shackleton and the king's brother-in-law, the Duke of Argyll, and thus the monarch was anxious to stop all rumours and press speculation. Despite royal intervention, a smear campaign had already begun against Sir Arthur Vicars, on nationalist anti-Dublin Castle grounds, just like the earlier campaign against Cornwall. Dungan reports that Sir Anthony McDonnell, Undersecretary for Ireland, had a brother in the Irish Parliamentary Party and he circulated a report that 'there was a connection between Vicars and a group of homosexuals in London'.[44] The jewels were never recovered and Vicars and Shackleton were dismissed, but the Irish Crown jewels scandal still made its way into public discussion, with the *Gaelic American Journal* asserting that 'Mr Shackleton's whole private life was turned inside out – evidence of his disgusting misconduct was dragged to light . . . Sodom and Gomorrah were destroyed by fire but Dublin Castle still stands.'[45] Again, homophobia could be counted on when the politics of the public scandal dictated.

My contention is that, in Ireland, Wilde largely escaped the full rigours of widespread condemnation experienced in Britain and the United States. He himself fully understood the consequences of his public 'outing', his martyrdom. When it was proposed in 1898 that *The Ballad of Reading Gaol* be published anonymously, he commented: 'As regards America, it would be better now to publish there without my name. I see it is my name that terrifies.'[46] As a result of an intensification of cultural nationalism into the early twentieth century, Wilde's appearances in the Old Bailey, his downfall and his sexual crime could be reinterpreted by later Irish writers in the light of their own aesthetic and political purposes, creating a much different 'Wilde century' in Ireland. Wilde's name seemed never to terrify anyone in Ireland.

2. Nationalising Wilde:
1900–1928

> How far and in what ways the dissemination of the Wildean queer images might apply to Ireland needs a lot more investigation. (Alan Sinfield)[1]

The years after Wilde's death in 1900 and up to the foundation and consolidation of the new Irish state in the late 1920s constituted a period of intense debate over political self-definition in Ireland, as outlined, for example, by Lucy McDiarmid in her study *The Irish Art of Controversy*.[2] I argue in this chapter that Wilde's reputation and the contestation of his racial and sexual identity became part of this larger debate, this moment of national remaking, and I examine the ways in which he became nationalised as Wilde the Irish rebel. R.F. Foster writes that,

> The Boer War at the beginning of the century focused much moderate Irish opinion into an anti-imperial mould and provided a mobilising 'cause' against the government; the European War of 1914–18 altered the condition of Irish politics beyond recognition. The radicalisation of Irish politics (and to a certain extent, of Irish society) took place between these two events and largely because of them.[3]

Wilde's posthumous reputation was implicated in this radicalisation, to his benefit.

In England after the trials, as Alan Sinfield notes, Wilde's name had become forbidden and silenced, and yet, somehow, he was made even more visible by virtue of being silenced. On perceptions of Wilde's sexuality in retrospect, Sinfield observes:

> 'The Wilde Trial had done its work', Carpenter wrote, 'and silence must henceforth reign on sex-subjects'. However, it was a Wilde-shaped silence. *The Echo* wrote: 'The best thing for everybody now is to forget all about Oscar Wilde, his perpetual posings, his aesthetical teachings and his theatrical productions. Let him go into silence, and be heard of no more.' But of course, this very injunction is reproducing Wilde.[4]

In Ireland in the years after his death, as I will show, Wilde was far from invisible, with productions of his plays in mainstream theatres, reviews of his writings and mentions in the national newspapers, as well as in interviews and memoirs. Most striking was the way in which Wilde was commandeered by fellow Anglo-Irish writers to become part of a particular tradition of Irish nationalist discourse.

In the first decades of the twentieth century, Wilde was 'nationalised' (a phrase from Margot Norris)[5], that is, claimed as a figure of transgressive aesthetic empowerment by Yeats, Joyce, Shaw and other Anglo-Irish writers central to debates about Irish cultural nationalism in this period. My argument in this chapter is that Wilde came to be read by subsequent Irish writers as heroic in his disruptive 'sinfulness', a figure of anti-colonial resistance; and this reconstruction in some ways mitigated his aberrant homosexuality for those writers and indeed for their society. This process of nationalisation derived partly from James Joyce, writing in 1909 in Trieste to celebrate the poet of Salome as the prophet of sin, and partly from the accounts of Shaw and Yeats casting Wilde as the tragic hero. Wilde became a figure of profound emblematic and aesthetic empowerment for both Joyce and Yeats and thus was a powerful shadow for the two most influential Irish writers of the twentieth century. Wilde's contemporary, Shaw, cited his Anglo-Irish pride as a key support for his heroic stance, and, when *The Importance of Being Earnest* was staged in the Abbey Theatre in 1926, Lady Augusta Gregory reflected in her journals on Wilde's poetry and on his tragic stature. His Protestant Anglo-Irish identity became an important protection for his homosexuality, as it was intertwined in these accounts with his mother's status as a nationalist poet. Common to many of these accounts of Oscar the Irish rebel is a need to situate his homosexuality within discourses of Anglo-Irish feudal pride, and Speranza, Lady Wilde, is seen as central to any account of Oscar the rebel. Indeed, throughout this book, I will examine the ways in which Irish writers portray not only Wilde himself but also central figures in Wilde's life, like Speranza, Bosie, his wife Constance, and suggest that, as Ireland changes, so do representations of Wilde and of those closest to him. The whole saga of his upbringing, his marriage and his homosexuality is reinterpreted in light of the political and cultural position of Irish biographers and commentators.

This, therefore, was a cultural moment in Ireland where Wilde could be claimed by some as a rebel, but it was a temporary moment. His name was gradually shifted from mainstream discourse, particularly after the foundation of the Irish state in 1922, by the increasing conservatism of the largely Catholic political majority from the late 1920s onwards. By the 1930s, those writers who had validated Wilde in the aftermath of his trials were those who found themselves outside the centres of power in the new Irish state. Within an independent Irish state, Wilde's Anglo-Irish pride and his homosexuality were moved to the margin. Wilde would be nation-alised only for a brief period.

However, some elements of this notion of Wilde the martyr continued into twentieth-century Ireland and beyond into contemporary Ireland and I will be discussing the writings of Seamus Heaney, Tom Paulin and Bernard O'Donoghue in later chapters. For now, I would make the point that, however attractive it is to see Wilde as an emblem for sexual rebel-lion, this is a trope that needs to be approached carefully. Lucy McDiarmid usefully disagrees with this trend within Wildean discourse in Ireland. She argues that: 'The Irish rebel paradigm is the wrong para-digm for Wilde, however'.[6] Her counter-argument is that Wilde never used the established language of the nineteenth-century Irish patriot, and, in particular, never sought death or martyrdom in the interests of his actual cause, his legal challenge to the Marquis of Queensberry. Rather, McDiarmid interprets Wilde as part of another tradition. This she calls 'Oppositional celebrities'[7] like Byron and others, who sought to disrupt the certainties and conformities of middle-class and upper-class society with a transgressive aesthetic of rebellious, anti-bourgeois literary stances. In a memorable phrase, McDiarmid argues that, for Wilde, 'It's not *Tiocfaidh ár Lá* but *épater le bourgeois*'.[8] (My own sense is that Wilde's self-presentation during the trials veered between two stances. He had occasional moments of outrageous wit and daring homoerotic play, as opposed to 'the love that dare not speak its name' speech, the attempt to make homosexuality sexless, intellectual and thus moral and aesthetic.)[9]

McDiarmid also suggests that Wilde was deploying a late-Victorian ideology of Hellenistic (and homoerotic) art to justify and defend his same-sex activities as platonic, and he never resorted to an Irish Republican genealogy or language as a resistance to blame and censure. Conversely, in McDiarmid's view, Irish Republicans 'defiantly and pub-licly accepted responsibility for their actions'.[10] She goes on: 'But where the Irish patriots accepted the higher criminality of their militant nation-alism, Wilde defined his "love" in a way that insists on his innocence.'[11] She argues that, unlike Wilde and other oppositional celebrities, Irish rebels were sexual conformists, conservative and well-behaved in their domestic lives. In terms of self-perception and public self-presentation, Irish nationalism and sexual rebellion were, it seems, incompatible. (As I suggest later on in this chapter, such an alliance between sexual rebellion and Irish nationalism seemed possible for Joyce, Yeats and Casement.) In short, McDiarmid suggests that Wilde had very little sense that he was offering himself for sacrifice when he took the case against Queensberry: 'The Wilde family tradition valorised a proud and defiant stance in the dock but there were no family martyrs . . . Speranza spoke the language of patriotism, but in her own life, style and celebrity had always sufficed.'[12] McDiarmid makes the shrewd observation that it was the Mary Travers libel case of 1864 and not the Charles Gavan Duffy trial that offered Wilde an exemplar of his family's relationship with the law. McDiarmid concludes her argument by suggesting that:' 'Slowly, gradually, after his release, Wilde began to speak with a different consciousness of the trials' meaning. Retrospectively, he shaped his experiences to fit the religious paradigm from which the Irish paradigm takes its shape: "I shall now live as the Infamous St Oscar of Oxford, Poet and Martyr", he wrote to Robbie Ross in 1898.'[13] McDiarmid's summation of Wilde's own motives for taking the case against Queensberry and his own sense of purpose and identification during the trials is a compelling one and it is only afterwards that Wilde's name became associated with the tradition of the Irishman beleaguered in the dock of an English courtroom.

Margot Backus considers that 'In Joyce's 1909 Triestene essay "Oscar Wilde: The Poet of Salome" however, Wilde's general makeover from English pervert to Irish martyr, while certainly inaccurate is both complex and revealing',[14] and she sees his essay on Wilde as signifying 'a space of unrepresentability that Irish culture and homosexuals share relative to mainstream British scandal culture'.[15] The Wilde that Joyce celebrates in this essay is simply a 'heroised' version of himself and, as Backus comments, 'Joyce's transfusion of wild Irishness into his representation of Wilde is thus an ostentatiously textual construct, stemming from a particular agenda of Joyce's connected to his own self-representation as a persecuted artist liable to be silenced and dismissed owing to his Irish subject position.'[16] Backus argues that, as a result, references to the Wilde trials underpin *Ulysses* as much as the Parnell divorce case, and supply Joyce with a crucial metaphor for an idea of scandal in the Circe episode of *Ulysses*, a point not much noticed in Joycean criticism. She makes a very useful distinction between those conservative mainstream Irish Catholic nationalists who didn't want to engage with Wilde and with Wildean sin, and those writers such as Yeats, Shaw and Joyce who promoted Wilde as a nationalist to redefine an Ireland whose right to independence they all asserted in terms more congenial to themselves as artists.[17] Broadly speaking, Backus's view that Wilde was uncongenial as an emblematic figure for conservative nationalists, particularly in the new Irish state, is supported by the account of his cultural presence in Ireland in later chapters of this study. It seems as if those writers who claimed Wilde up to and after the creation of the New Ireland were somehow liminal to that Ireland, as dissident artists, as Anglo-Irish and/or Protestant, or as sexually other. One of the very few exceptions is the Irish cultural nationalist Daniel Corkery, an opponent of foreign or 'un-Irish' art. Yet Corkery quotes Wilde approvingly in his study of Gaelic poetry, *The Hidden Ireland*.[18] Otherwise, Wilde is never part of mainstream Irish cultural discourse – those who do cite him do so from a point of distance or marginality, either sexually or culturally.

As with Britain, Wilde's name became a byword for a criminalised sexuality, particularly in cases of police harassment regarding same-sex activities between men. Diarmaid Ferriter, in his book *Occasions of Sin*, tells of a court case in April 1903 where a 32-year-old man was accused of attempted buggery with a young soldier on February 1903. In the police deposition, the soldier alleged 'That's the man that tried to Oscar Wilde me and he gave me money and drink to get me out of the house and he told me to come back tomorrow night and he's give me plenty more'.[19] In spite of persistent police harassment of men having sex with other men in Ireland, Wilde continued to have a visible presence in popular culture in Ireland in the immediate aftermath of his disgrace, which did not happen in Britain. For example, there were five productions of his plays in Ireland between 1900 and 1928, with two productions in Belfast's Grand Opera House, in 1900 and 1901. Likewise, the Abbey Theatre had two productions of his work, *The Importance of Being Earnest* in 1926 and *Salome* in 1928.[20] In addition, despite the trials and their aftermath, Wilde could be written about in the most unexpected of contexts in Ireland. In 1905, a retired priest, L.C.P. Fox, wrote a long, gossipy series of articles for the Catholic journal *Donahoe's* entitled 'People I Have Met'. In one article, Fox made much of his friendship with Speranza during Wilde's childhood. Fox, born an English Quaker, converted to Catholicism as a young man and then became superior of the reformatory at Glencree, County Wicklow, where, he claimed, he had befriended Lady Wilde in the 1860s. In a conservative Catholic journal full of pious essays and articles, he writes openly about baptising her children Willie and Oscar in 1862 or 1863. 'I'm not sure whether she ever became a Catholic but it was not long before she asked me to instruct those two children, one of them being that future erratic genius Oscar Wilde. After a few weeks I baptized these two children, Lady Wilde herself being present on the occasion.'[21] H. Montgomery Hyde casts doubt on this alleged baptism, a part of accepted Wildean popular legend, pointing out that he could find no record of this event in the baptismal register of the church in Glencree during this period.

The Irish Times had many references to Wilde from the early 1900s onwards. Some of these were sympathetic, a review in the books page on 21 December 1906 referring to Wilde as 'that unhappy genius'.[22] The unnamed reviewer of a book about Wilde by Leonard Ingleby, published in 1907, is more forthright in his or her condemnation. Discussing Walter

Pater's educational influence on Wilde, the reviewer said that he or she believed that this education 'bore terrible fruit . . . Mr Ingleby is disposed to argue that the criminal side of him [Wilde] was only part of his complex nature'. The reviewer goes on to suggest that Wilde's criminality should always be kept in mind and seen as part of his overall personality.[23] In *Notable Irishwomen*, a study published in 1909, C.J. Hamilton claimed to have known Speranza and said indirectly of Oscar that 'the last years of her life were clouded by trouble into which there is no need to enter here'.[24] Here, an example of a Wilde-shaped silence. Between 1910 and 1912, Dublin University Dramatic Society performed three Wilde comedies, all these performances reviewed and admired in the newspapers. In *The Irish Times* in 1911, the books page carried a long review of a new edition of Wilde's poems which argued that, in Wilde's earlier poetry, he 'cannot claim to be considered a great poet, he does not experience an emotion, he describes it', but the reviewer goes on to argue that prison and the attendant suffering humanised him and thus made Wilde into a real, feeling poet, and that *The Ballad of Reading Gaol* and *De Profundis* are his only mature writings.[25] In 1913 *The Irish Times* carried a review of Thurston Hopkins's book on Wilde, where the reviewer concluded, sympathetically and astutely that 'His was distinctly a remarkable genius, perverted in some degrees, misunderstood in others, the object of extravagant praises and extravagant blame. . . . It is a valuable introduction to an understanding of Wilde's character and work.'[26] Further evidence of interest in Wilde can be seen in the 1915 review of Stuart Mason's bibliography of Wilde's writings, which concluded that 'It is not yet too late for us, as Irishmen, to feel proud that our age produced such plays as these.'[27]

Sometimes an absence of any discussion of Wilde can have its own significance. Padraig Pearse was clearly influenced by Wilde's poems and by his stories, in particular 'The Selfish Giant' and 'The Happy Prince', in some of his writings for children. However, Pearse never directly acknowledged this influence, as Elaine Sisson comments in her study *Pearse's Patriots*:

> Lack of documentary evidence and the limitations of research methodologies make it impossible to determine whether Pearse practised or thought about same-sex relationships. Given his orthodox Catholic background, his highly principled, highly disciplined life and the sheltered conservative social circles in which he moved, it seems highly unlikely that Pearse envisaged the possibility of sexual relations between men. The trial and death of Oscar Wilde happened within Pearse's adult life, yet there is no mention of any of Pearse's papers, although it seems unlikely that he could have been unaware of Wilde's fate.[28]

Pearse never wrote directly of Wilde, but his writings reflect a connection around the configuration of the homoerotic, a connection that Pearse seems to have been unable to acknowledge. Susan C. Harris, in her study *Gender and Modern Irish Drama*,[29] analyses Pearse's representations of the homoerotic in a chapter called 'Excess of Love: Padraig Pearse and the Erotics of Sacrifice' and identifies the connections between Irish Republican ideology and the aesthetics of male sacrifice in his plays. Harris makes the point that, in the years after the Wilde trials and leading up to the 1916 Easter Rising, the nineteenth-century concept of a female Ireland in flight from a male aggressor, Britain, was becoming less viable because of male Irish Republican anxieties about any perceived female weakness and passivity. Instead, in nationalist newspapers, ballads and dramas, like those written by Pearse for his school St Enda's, the battle between British imperialism and Irish nationalism was being re-gendered as a masculine one, the struggle between two equal males, and therefore the aesthetic of homoerotic conflict and sacrifice became central to Pearse's Republican writings. Harris suggests that, 'Like Pearse's political speeches, his sacrificial plays show how and why the story of the male martyr's self-sacrifice became so important to him.'[30] Wilde's own writings are filled with images of male sacrifice and suicide, of beautiful St Sebastian figures, but Pearse never dared make explicit any such link. Wilde attempted to make his own homosexuality acceptable by claiming that it was platonic, Hellenic and asexual. Pearse transmuted his own forbidden, unsettling and disturbing erotic attraction towards his young male pupils by making that erotic attraction part of his desexualised ritual of patriotic sacrifice. Harris argues that,

> In order to make the argument for revolution possible, republican writers had to redefine the concept of masculinity for Irish men; that this redefinition highlighted the instability and incoherence of sexual identity in a way that was profoundly disturbing; and that Pearse's experience with sublimating his own sexual desires translated into a version of the sacrificial paradigm that helped keep that construct of masculinity together.[31]

Clearly Wilde directly influenced Pearse's stories for children and indirectly influenced his notion of aesthetic sacrifice, but neither influence was safe or permissible for Pearse to acknowledge and so he is silent about Wilde, presumably uneasy about acknowledging any possible connection with the notoriously homosexual outcast.

Likewise, Wilde is a significant absence for another Irish Republican who wrote of the homoerotic, Roger Casement. Like Pearse, Casement also fails to mention the Wilde trials in all of his writings, particularly in his diaries, but his silence is eloquent given what we now know about his own hidden sexual life. Parallels between these two famously homosexual Irishmen are revealing and many links have been established between the two men, with a recent Casement biographer, Jeffrey Dudgeon, comparing him with Wilde as 'another Irish Protestant whose life patterns and national sympathies were remarkably similar, Oscar Wilde'.[32] Susan C. Harris links the two figures by suggesting that:

> In 1916 homosexuality was thoroughly pathologised; to have suggested then that Pearse felt the same desire that Casement's diaries recorded could only have had the effect of discrediting both him and the republican cause. But that climate of homophobia did not arise spontaneously out of some essential and unchanging 'natural' human disgust for homosexuality; it was produced and maintained by cultural forces that were more powerful then than now. Eighty-five years later the power of that discourse has weakened enough to allow us to discuss Pearse's sexuality without maligning his character.[33]

Casement's sexuality, unlike that of Pearse, had always been discussed in Ireland, to such an extent that Lucy McDiarmid suggests in her essay 'The Afterlife of Roger Casement' that 'Casement is not just a curiosity for writers: he is a persistent presence in popular culture'[34] and this lively afterlife, detailed with great skill by McDiarmid, meant that his homosexuality was argued and contested by those wishing to retain his heroic Republican status. This continuous engagement by modern Ireland with Casement and with his so-called Black Diaries contrasts sharply with the evasions and silences around Wilde's homosexuality. Why was this? Partly, Casement remained central to Irish public discourse throughout the twentieth century because his homosexuality was in doubt; maybe his diaries were forged by enemies of Irish Republicanism. Moreover, Casement's commitment to the cause of Irish freedom was unequivocal; Wilde was, at best, a doubtful patriot. So Casement's visibility, when contrasted with Wilde's ambiguous status, confirms that homosexuality could form part of mainstream Irish cultural discourse only when it can be made subordinate to Irish nationalism.

Another middle-class Catholic of this period, James Joyce, was a key figure in reconstructions of Wilde and his fate. Joyce's appropriation of Wilde as a symbolic figure of sin and dissidence is a vital one for Wilde's presence in twentieth-century Ireland. Catholic by upbringing and education, Joyce was thirteen when Wilde's trials took place and eighteen when Wilde died, and so his view of Wilde is constructed very much at a distance, both temporally and spatially. In March 1909, Joyce published an article called 'Oscar Wilde: The Poet of Salome' in a newspaper in

Trieste to mark a performance of Richard Strauss's opera *Salome*. In this article, the question of Wilde's homosexuality is tackled directly with Joyce's characteristic forthrightness, and is made possible only because he was writing outside Ireland. In discussing Wilde's sexuality, Joyce opens with a dubious genetic rationalisation for Wilde's sexual nature, suggesting an epileptic personality as a causal factor for his homosexuality without supplying any corroborating biographical evidence. Furthermore Joyce cites, again without evidence, the idea that Speranza wished for a daughter while she was pregnant with Oscar and then dressed her younger son in skirts, *dragging* (my italics) him to his ruin, as a determining factor for his evolving sexuality.[35] (There is no evidence for this; Wilde was dressed in petticoats, as were all Victorian boys, and Speranza delighted in having two sons, as her letters from this period attest.) In these unconsciously misogynistic early accounts, Speranza is usually cited as the cause of Wilde's degeneration, seemingly without much care for biographical or psychological accuracy, and this will occur again and again in later Irish writings on Wilde.

However, Joyce moves on to make the much more radical point that Wilde destabilised the widespread homosocial structures underpinning Victorian British male culture by bringing his sexuality into the open, however unwittingly. Joyce identifies precisely the homophobic panic that Wilde's 'outing' unleashed in the male social structures of his time:[36] The consequent rage against Wilde in Britain was the rage of a society recognising itself.[37] At this very early stage, Joyce was making the enlightened point that homophobia is produced as a support and a counter-discourse against which heterosexuality can define itself and thus assure itself of its own naturalness and centrality.

The imaginative need of the exiled Joyce was to see Wilde as an artist who challenged the political and moral hegemony of the British Empire; Joyce begets him, as it were, as a precursor for his own aesthetic of exile, disgrace and defiance. Again, there is little sense of Wilde's actual motives in bringing the case against Queensberry; merely a kind of retroactive mythologising in the light of Joyce's own aesthetic needs. Joyce saw Wilde as a kind of high priest of sin and neo-paganism.[38] Thus Joyce saw Wilde as an exemplar, refashioned in his own likeness as a subversive and a rebel, affording him both a counter-tradition of Irish dissent and also an attack against Ireland and Britain.

Other critics have observed the opportunity offered in Wilde's fate for Joyce's rebellion against the constraints of his own country and the very partial Joycean versions of Wilde. Joseph Valente writes:

> Mediated by his compatriot Wilde, Oxford Hellenism afforded Joyce a
> script to be performed or mimicked in his youth and a narrative code

to be implemented and manipulated in his fictive representations of that youth. It lent the lived and the written story a shared ideological basis, a discourse of individual freedom and self-development that could address and resist in concerted fashion the main intellectual, sexual and aesthetic constraints of Irish catholic life and the political inequalities of British colonial rule.[39]

The importance of Joyce's version of Wilde, however, is the link made between the institutional homophobia at the centre of the trials and a critique of British imperialism, and this would provide later Irish writers with an acceptable way in which to reclaim Wilde.

Perhaps the two most influential Irish sources of biographical detail on Wilde come from his contemporaries Yeats and Shaw. In many ways, Yeats is the most important interpreter of Wilde and the one whose dramatic writings are most strongly influenced by his example. Their very particular views of Wilde were to shape Irish popular and cultural perceptions up to the present. W.B. Yeats, in his 1914 autobiography, writes warmly of his friendship with the older writer and acknowledges the importance of his aesthetic influence and helpful patronage on his arrival in London in the late 1880s. Yeats's later dramatic writings owed much to Wilde, particularly *Salome*. Crucially for later Irish biographies, Yeats's account deals with his support for Wilde and his visit to Willie Wilde's house in May 1895, during the third trial, when the young poet was anxious to assist Wilde with letters of support from other Irish writers.

Yeats's reaction to Wilde's disgrace was one of enlightened sympathy and support. Although he hoped that Wilde was innocent of the charges of sexual immorality, he valorised his sense of manliness.[40] Many of Yeats's closest friends and associates in London at this time were either homosexual or bisexual and so the public exposure of Wilde's same-sex activities did not unduly bother him. Like Joyce, Yeats was much more concerned with reconstructing Wilde as the archetype of the Irish tragic artist, the lone figure standing against the commonplace, and as a result suffering martyrdom at the hands of oversexualised heterosexuals.[41] Yeats, like Joyce, thus made problematic the very heterosexuality that stigmatised Wilde as sexual 'other'. Yeats is also the only source, and a vague one at that, for the story that Lady Wilde urged her son to stay and face prison rather than leave for France. This otherwise unattested story has become part of the Wilde legend, the Irish rebel mother urging her son to live up to the code of Irish Republican honour. [42] As a result, in later Irish accounts of Wilde like that of Terry Eagleton, Speranza's maternal influence is seen as a central causal factor for explanations of Wilde's sexuality and as a driving force in his journey towards public disgrace and consequent aesthetic martyrdom. In these accounts of Wilde's aberrant sexuality, Speranza's Republicanism is always validated and honoured, and thus used to compensate for what was perceived as her over-whelming, damaging maternal influence. Up to recently, the usual misconception of the formulation of the homosexual man was that a close relationship with a mother feminised a son and made him unmanly; i.e. sexually other. Thus, unfairly, Speranza's warm and consistently supportive relationship with her son is reconstructed as a factor in Wilde's sexuality and thus in his disgrace.[43] Later in his life, Yeats told Wilde's biographer, H. Montgomery Hyde, that

> The rage against Wilde . . . was also complicated by the Britisher's jealousy of art and the artist, which is generally dormant but is called into activity when the artist has got outside his field into publicity of an undesirable kind. This hatred is not due to any action of the artist or eminent man; it is merely the expression of an individual hatred and envy, become collective because circumstances have made it so.[44]

Wilde's fellow Anglo-Irish Protestant writer Bernard Shaw has left a very different but equally influential version of the same events. Shaw provided a letter of commentary in 1916 for his friend Frank Harris's biography of Wilde and this letter was later published as part of Harris's study. Shaw was a contemporary of Wilde's growing up in Dublin and perhaps the two men were rather too close for comfort as Irish writers in London. Shaw was characteristically sceptical about Wilde's aesthetic and sexual proclivities,[45] but he did have a profound insight into Wilde's comedies of manners, seeing them as part of the tradition of Anglo-Irish dramatic writing in London. Joseph Bristow points out that Shaw was the first critic to note the connection between Wilde's Irishness and the subversive subtext of his comedies.[46]

However, when Wilde became the subject of widespread public opprobrium in London, Shaw, like Yeats, supported Wilde and tried to dissuade him from taking the libel case against Queensberry, much to Bosie's fury. Shaw displays supportive broad-mindedness, but also distance and self-doubt when writing to Harris about Wilde's homosexuality.[47] However, Shaw found it necessary to comment on Wilde's homosexuality in such a way as to distance himself from an understanding of homosexuality, and here again Speranza is found to be at fault.[48]

In his letter, Shaw seeks a biological explanation for Wilde's so-called aberrant sexuality by expounding the startling theory that his mother, Lady Wilde, was suffering from an abnormal physical condition called gigantism and that Wilde had inherited her physical abnormality and was thus sexually monstrous. Shaw offers no medical proof for this theory, apart from the evidence of his own eyes. However, he clearly feels the need to explain away the sexuality that led Wilde to prison, seeing the grotesque body of the mother as the perverting influence on normative heterosexuality. (Shaw was a regular at Speranza's London soirées and he repaid her kindness with acknowledgement but also with this comic portrayal.) This theory became commonplace in later biographies, even a reputable one of Hyde's. At the end of his letter to Harris, Shaw falls back on the code of Anglo-Irish feudal honour to justify Wilde's stance, believing that his Irish pride meant he refused to run away from his trial.[49] This Anglo-Irish pride seems to cleanse Wilde of his sexual shame.

One of Shaw's most stubborn, if whimsically expressed, beliefs was in the moral strength and tenacity of Irish Protestants, as compared to their English or American counterparts, and it is with this vindication of his own class, the Irish Protestant, that Shaw finishes his account of Wilde:

> Please let us hear no more of the tragedy of Oscar Wilde . . . Oscar was no tragedian. He was the superb comedian of his century, on to whom misfortune, disgrace, imprisonment were external and traumatic. His gaiety of soul was invulnerable: it shines through the blackest pages of *De Profundis* as clearly as his funniest epigrams. Even on his deathbed he found in himself no pity for himself, playing for the laugh with his last breath, and getting it with as sure a stroke as in his palmiest prime.[50]

Seamus Deane comments that, 'Between them, Yeats and Joyce recognise in Wilde the first Irish writer in whom the tragic plight of the modern artist is fully represented. More effectively than Shaw, he embodied in his life and his art contradictions by which he was victimised, and, at the same time, stimulated . . . Yeats learnt from and emulated him in this respect.'[51]

A close friend of both Yeats and Shaw, the Abbey playwright and Anglo-Irish writer Augusta Gregory had met Wilde at London dinner parties in the late 1880s. In September 1887, Wilde asked her to write for his journal, *Woman's World*. She mentions Wilde many times in her later diaries and always Yeats is her source for Wildean gossip and lore.[52]

Yeats was often Gregory's source on Wilde, and her comments are always full of admiration for a man whose fate she found intensely moving, a heroic figure in the mould of the courageous Anglo-Irish code to which honour she aspired. She writes in her diary in December 1928 of rereading old letters from Yeats to herself about Wilde and remembering stories of Wilde dying in agony but with great heroism.[53] Later in the same entry she calls *The Ballad of Reading Gaol*, 'A wonderful indictment of what horrible chastisement man can inflict on man'.[54]

The Ballad of Reading Gaol found another admirer, an Irishman in an English prison, albeit it from the perspective of Irish militant

Republicanism. In May 1916, Michael Collins wrote to his sister from Staffordshire Detention Barracks quoting Wilde. Collins's biographer, Tim Pat Coogan, records that Wilde had been a favourite author of Collins during his time working in London in 1909. In this prison letter, Collins writes, 'Positively you have no idea of what it's like, the dreadful monotony, the heart-scalding eternal brooding on all sorts of things . . . Wilde's "Reading Gaol" keeps coming up. You remember "all that we know/ Who be in gaol".'[55] Collins, known primarily for his heterosexual love affairs, nevertheless felt an affinity with this imprisoned Irishman. His recent biographer, Peter Hart, makes the point that:

> What we know for sure of Collins's romantic relationships with women is quite conventional. Of course, as with the rest of humanity, what we know is dwarfed by what we do not and never will. Did he sleep with admirers or employees – or with his fiancée? Did he ever share sexual experiences with male friends? Since opportunities and urges to do at least some of these things undoubtedly existed, as did vast amounts of hypocrisy on the part of respectable people in general (pious republicans included), it would be hardly surprising if one or more of these things happened.[56]

Wilde's name was still being associated, although somewhat uneasily in the opening years of the twentieth century, with his native city in travel guides and books about Dublin's literary and cultural heritage. For example, D.L. Kay (D.L. Kelleher), in his 1918 guide *The Glamour of Dublin*, writes under this entry on Merrion Square:

> Here at the north-western corner in that house with the glass gallery along its second floor lived an Irishman, immortal now by many tests, son of Sir William and Lady Wilde, a 'child of decay', one Oscar, at whose birth, they say, the exotics in the glass-house drooped . . . And this poet-pale young fellow, six feet high, with the intensely supercilious mouth and an abominable condescension in the set of his chin . . . Oscar Fingal O'Flaherty Wilde, maniac and artist, the most distinguished outcast after MacMurrough that Dublin has ever yet known.[57]

Like Yeats, Gregory and Shaw, the playwright Sean O'Casey sought to valorise his fellow Irish Protestant. In an interview in the *Freeman's Journal* in 1924, O'Casey's debt to Wilde is acknowledged by the interviewer:

> Translations of French works helped him toward self-expression. For there is something more Gallic than Gaelic in the quality of his mind. He is a great admirer of the works of Oscar Wilde. 'Wilde was not evil,' he says indignantly, 'he was made so by the world around him. One sees the real Wilde in his writings as one sees the disgusting playmakers of the English Restoration period in theirs.'[58]

While Irish Protestant writers found Wilde to be courageous and a man who was prepared to stand and fight, Catholic writers continued to find in his imprisonment and life afterwards an example of punishment, repentance and the finding of a true humility. The *Connacht Tribune* in 1926 carried a lecture by the Reverend Dr Pearse of Maynooth, who spoke at University College Galway on the subject of 'Catholic social science' where Wilde is remade as an exemplar of Catholic belief:

> Who are we, creatures of a day, that we can understand the eternal plan? This we know that pain has its uses in enriching and deepening experience. Thus we know that Oscar Wilde was changed from a flippant, cynical writer to an earnest and impassioned poet by *Reading Gaol* and could then speak of broken hearts resembling the fragrant alabaster box that Mary broke for her Lord.[59]

Finally, some sense of the uneasy heritage of Wilde's name in Dublin at this period can be gleaned from this story, told in 'The Irishman's Diary' of *The Irish Times* of 1954,[60] going back to the première of Alla Nazimova's 1923 film version of *Salome*,[61] which opened in Dublin in October 1924. The diarist writes:

> But this story I can vouch for. In the early years of the century, a primitive film of Wilde's *Salome* was made and shown in Dublin . . . Dublin was plastered with lurid posters advertising this feature but although the Corporation was prepared to turn a blind eye on a scantily clad Salome, they drew the line at that man's name in any of the publicity. So men with buckets of paste were sent out to cover up the words 'By Oscar Wilde' with neat little rectangles of white paper on the poster.[62]

However, as the diarist tells us, the rain washed away all the little rectangles of white paper and the forbidden name was again made visible. Wilde's name proved un-erasable. In the years to come, Wilde's name refused to stay censored and would not be invisible.

3. Wilde in the new Irish state: 1930–1960

In this chapter, I trace Wilde's presence within the emergent Irish state at a crucial time of a cultural programme of self-invention and nation building. Ireland had achieved political autonomy in 1922 and what was being gradually constructed in the late 1920s and into the 1930s was an official or state version of the idea of 'Irishness'. This national identity actively supported and promoted the ideal of linguistic, economic and cultural self-sufficiency as a necessary adjunct to political independence and had a certain idealism inherited from earlier revolutionary times. It has been argued that, as a result, intellectually and culturally Ireland became stagnant in the late 1930s and 1940s, with what Terence Brown describes as 'the devastating lack of cultural and social innovation in the first decade of Irish independence.[1] He goes on to state that 'an explanation for this social and cultural conservatism of the new state is, I believe, to be sought and not found in the social composition of Irish society'.[2] Maria Luddy notes that 'the process of Irish independence was disruptive in a number of ways: traditional ideas about gender were challenged to a greater extent than ever before by the advance of the suffrage campaign'[3]

With the building of an overwhelmingly Catholic state of twenty-six counties, the sense was that all the radicalism of the previous decades was now gone. R.F. Foster argues that 'The rigorous conservatism of the Irish Free State has become a cliché; what matters most about the atmosphere and mentality of the twenty-six county Ireland in the 1920s is that the dominant preoccupation of the regime was self-definition against Britain – cultural and political.'[4] The Cork novelist and short-story writer Frank O'Connor puts it this way:

> After the success of the Revolution . . . Irish society began to revert to type. All the forces that had made for national dignity, that had united Catholic and Protestant aristocrats like Constance Markievicz, Labour revolutionaries like Connolly and writers like AE [George Russell], began to disintegrate, and Ireland became more than ever sectarian, utilitarian, the two nearly always go together, vulgar and provincial . . . Every year that has passed, particularly since de Valera's rise to power, has strengthened the grip of the gombeen man, of the religious secret societies like the Knights of Columbanus, of the illiterate censorships.[5]

Thus, the consolidation of the idea of an Irish republic led, amongst other measures, to the introduction of censorship in 1926 and this has been seen as an intensification of Catholic influence on the idea of an Irish state. But was it? Undoubtedly, censorship in Ireland had one target, the expression and depiction of sexuality. Tom Ingles writes that 'The inculcation of Victorian prudery throughout Irish society was not a universal or homogeneous process. It was a strategy of a new class of tenant farmer that emerged in the social space between the peasantry and the Protestant ascendancy class.'[6] This inculcation of prudery meant that the eroticised body, in any form, was absent from public discourse, yet during the Wilde trials his body had become the site for his unmentionable crime. Cheryl Herr comments on this disappearance of the body in Irish culture thus: 'Most writers on Ireland sooner or later put forward one trait that they see as definitive of the "Irish mind" or the "Celtic consciousness" . . . But one feature that almost no one mentions is the relationship between the Irish mind and any kind of Irish body.'[7] One result of the profound antipathy towards all public notions or acknowledgement of the body was a denial of the existence of homosexuality and so any discussion of homosexuality and of Wilde would be fraught with difficulty.

Yet the historian Diarmaid Ferriter raises the question as to the conservatism of de Valera's Ireland.

> From the perspectives of cynic's writings in the 1980s, it was 1930s oppression, and a failure to modernise, which meant that Ireland was simply not an interesting place to live in during this era. This, as Brian Fallon has recognised, ignores the degree of cultural vitality that continued to exist in Ireland; and just because this culture was imported does not mean that it should be ignored.[8]

This may be true, but the discourse of homosexuality presented a real challenge to the ideology of the new country. The question I want to consider is this one. Did Wilde's name present a difficulty in this period? The scant historical evidence shows that Ireland of the 1930s, 1940s and 1950s was indeed a time of repression and difficulty in relation to homosexuality. As Kieran Rose has shown: 'According to a government committee in the 1930s gross indecency between male persons was "spreading with malign vigour" and in 1946, a Labour Party report on Portlaoise prison stated that homosexuals constituted 30 per cent of the total and are kept apart from other prisoners.'[9] Diarmaid Ferriter in his book *Occasions of Sin* estimates that, for example, in the years 1928–9 there were eighty-six prosecutions and seventy-eight convictions for homosexual offences.[10]

Yet, despite this, productions of Wilde's plays continued to be staged in Ireland all through the 1930s and 1940s and Irish biographers and writers still found ways in which to write about Wilde and his sexuality, albeit some of these in the homophobic language of mainstream culture. Thus Wilde was not completely silenced in de Valera's Ireland. However, I would argue that he was muted or explained away, particularly in Irish Catholic circles.

In 1930 in a lecture to the Dublin Writers' Club, Katharine Tynan included Wilde and Speranza amongst 'famous people I have known'[11] and editions of his writings continued to be regularly reviewed throughout the 1930s in *The Irish Times*. On the other hand, as Owen Dudley Edwards recounts:

> Certainly various ecclesiastical authorities, lay and clerical, were pre-pared to discourage student productions of *The Importance of Being Earnest* up to the Second World War. Robert Donovan, in 1930, having been assigned licensing powers for student drama in his capacity as professor of English literature at University College Dublin, vetoed one such proposal as 'seeming to have the students go all out under the banner of Oscar Wilde'.[12]

One private moment in relation to Wilde is most revealing. In December 1935, Edith Somerville wrote to A.J.A. Symons in reply to his request for information on Oscar Wilde. Symons was researching a new biography of Wilde (never completed) and had written to Somerville asking for any memories she may have had of her contemporary Anglo-Irish writer. Her letter is courteous, but firm in denial of any personal acquaintanceship with Wilde. 'As to Oscar Wilde, I am sorry that Miss Hudson misled you as to my knowledge of him – I saw him once, on a bus in Paris and I made a (very indifferent) scribble of him, but tho' I have searched for it everywhere, I cannot find it – it has, however occurred to me that when Wilde was a very young man, he was very well known to a cousin of mine.'[13] (Somerville doesn't name this cousin but it may have been Bernard Shaw, married to her cousin Charlotte, and himself a close acquaintance of Wilde's.)

In a subsequent letter to Symons, Somerville continued to stress her complete lack of any first-hand acquaintanceship with Wilde. Nevertheless she supplied him with a slightly disdainful pen picture, given to her by an unnamed friend of the poet in his earlier years:

> I have been trying to keep my promise to find out what I could about Oscar Wilde – I'm sorry that I have not been more successful. His period is now rather remote and those living now were rather too young to have formed ideas about him. However one of my friends has given me a few recollections: he asks me not to mention his name but I know that you can trust the accuracy of his memory. He says:

> 'All I remember of OW in my childhood days was seeing him dance
> at my mother's house. We children called him the "wild sheep"
> because he looked like one! I knew him later in London and loathed
> shaking hands with his hot wet hand. The picture of him when I was
> a boy of seven or eight is vivid. I can't remember much of him later as
> I avoided him like poison.'[14]

This account is fascinating in its disingenuous distaste for Wilde (note the description of physical distaste). Edith, who was only four years younger than Wilde, lets it appear that she was of a younger generation and that she had never actually met him, apart from a sighting on a Paris bus. However, a much earlier letter to her partner Violet Martin tells a different tale.

In 1888 Edith Somerville was in London attempting to sell her stories and illustrations to various editors, and reports back on her meeting with the editor of *The Woman's World*:

> I went down to Oscar yesterday . . . He is a great fat oily beast . . . he
> pretended the most enormous interest . . . but it was all to no avail . . .
> He languidly took the sonnets and is to return them by post. He
> talked great rot that 'French subjects should be drawn by French
> artists' – I was near telling him, as Dr Johnson said: 'Who drives fat
> oxen must himself be fat.'[15]

Edith had indeed met him and, furthermore, it is clear from other letters that she and her partner understood much of the homoerotic subtexts of his writings. In 1890 Violet wrote to Edith on the subject of *The Picture of Dorian Gray*:

> Finished Dorian – which I think is a vulgar variation on Dr Jekyll –
> the only reason I can imagine your brother lending it to you is that
> he thought you wouldn't understand – if it is what I darkly surmise it
> to be, it is the most daring beastliness ever I struck – but keep this to
> yourself – certainly I would be afraid to own to having read it, to a
> man.[16]

Edith Somerville's attitude towards Wilde and her disclaiming of any personal connection is unusual, but understandable in her case, driven by a fear of sexual difference which might have reflected uncomfortably on her own earlier life partnership with the now deceased Violet Martin in this new Ireland.

An unusual citing of Wilde as literary influence came from Daniel Corkery in his *The Hidden Ireland* in 1941, a key text in the construction of Ireland's colonial history from the perspective of cultural nationalism in the Ireland of the 1940s. Corkery uses his study of eighteenth-century Gaelic poets to advance a utopian notion of a new Irish literature, an organic, national art that would transcend the 'taint' of colonisation and anglicisation and, in his introduction, he finds Wilde as an unexpected ally in his ideological battle. 'The antithesis of fifteenth–sixteenth century renaissance art in this regard is national art . . . The renaissance may have justified itself but not, we feel, either on the plane of genuine Christian art or genuine pagan art.' In a footnote, Corkery expands, 'While writing this, I had forgotten that Wilde had more brilliantly said the same thing.' Corkery goes on to quote *De Profundis*.[17]

Wilde's two alma maters in Ireland, Trinity College Dublin and Portora Royal School, Enniskillen, behaved with characteristic unease around the name of their infamous student. Interestingly, *The Irish Times* carried a report, 'A Revaluation of Oscar Wilde', in November 1937 of a paper read by a student, W.P.M. Ross, at the college Philosophical Society, called 'Oscar Wilde: An Impression'. In this paper, the student seems to absolve Trinity College from any blame in relation to Wilde's 'decadence' and his homosexuality. 'After a successful period at Trinity College, Dublin, Wilde went to Oxford, appearing as a dandy and becoming well-known as an eccentric.' The essay on Wilde ends with the judgement: 'Wilde's fall . . . was due to the fact that he ceased to create at a time when his mind was most alive, and he sought satisfaction in excess and perversion. Wilde knew that the satisfaction of the artist lay in his never being satisfied.'[18]

In the history of Trinity College Dublin by Constantia Maxwell,[19] Wilde is mentioned merely as a student of Mahaffy's, and, in a later history by K.C. Bailey in 1947, the author opined that 'The brilliant but degenerate author of *Lady Windermere's Fan* and *The Importance of Being Earnest* seems not to have found Trinity College altogether to his taste.'[20] By 1954, T.G. Wilson, biographer of Oscar's father Sir William Wilde, wrote in an essay for the medical journal *The Practitioner* called 'Oscar Wilde at Trinity',[21] a sympathetic account: 'Oscar Wilde, the centenary of whose birth occurs this month, has been the subject of much inaccurate writing since his death'. He goes on to argue, shrewdly distancing himself from homosexual 'sin', that 'most of the biographies which have been published have been biased, either on behalf or against Oscar. Few of them refer to his essential good nature and infectious charm of manner, qualities which he undoubtedly possessed and which have no relation to the deplorable misdeeds which eventually led to his spectacular downfall.'[22] Wilson's underlying effect in this essay is to distance and thus exonerate Trinity College Dublin from any hint of corrupting decadence by stressing Wilde's goodness and sexual reliability while still within its walls and his subsequent fall far away from his alma mater:

> The fatal weakness in his character did not appear until later; when it did, the majority of his friends from Trinity refused to have anything to do with him . . . It has often been said that had he lived in the present century, he would not have suffered as he did in expiation of his sins. This may be true in part but even the lax moral standards of today could not tolerate one who had sinned as blatantly as one who preached the gospel of decadence as assiduously as he did.[23]

A later history published by R.B. McDowell and D.A. Webb[24] in 1982 has only one reference to Wilde in relation to Mahaffy, and even J.V. Luce's 1992 *Trinity College Dublin: The First 400 Years*[25] mentions Wilde only in a footnote.

Trinity lecturer and gay activist David Norris, speaking during the same four-hundredth anniversary of the college, comments that

> Trinity College, indeed, has little to congratulate itself upon its attitude towards Wilde in his difficulty, Mahaffy in particular making the notorious remark 'we no longer speak of Mr Wilde' and refusing to be associated with a petition of clemency launched in 1896 although the honour of Trinity was somewhat redeemed by the signature on that petition of another distinguished classicist, Robert Yelverton Tyrell, professor of Latin.[26]

Likewise, in the history of Portora Royal School published in 1940, there is a brief mention of Wilde as having 'entered Trinity College Dublin in 1871 as a Royal scholar', but it tells us nothing else while including long descriptions of the career of other former Portorans.[27] In 1969, another Portora student, Samuel Beckett, won the Nobel Prize and in the press statement written by the headmaster's wife, Mary Rogers, she wrote that 'It was his [Beckett's] honesty perhaps that has made him disdain success and he had the example of that other Portora Oscar winner, Wilde who revelled in it and loved being lionised but hated and dreaded the work that were its preliminaries.'[28] David Norris in later, more enlightened times describes Wilde's time at Portora in these terms:

> He did brilliantly well at Portora winning many prizes and his name was consequently inscribed in the school's roll of honour. Following his conviction, however, in 1895, it was painted out and the initial which he carved on the classroom window scraped away by the headmaster. In recent years his repentant alma mater has regilded his name which gives it satisfactory prominence among his duller companions in glory.[29]

This ambivalence towards Wilde is clear in all kinds of cultural and literary sources for this time. For example, *Irish Travel*, which ran from 1925 to 1952, was a practical guide to holidaying, featuring hotel listings, suggested routes, and featuring overviews of towns, cities and counties. The only literary figure who appears with any regularity is Oliver Goldsmith, but still, there are many opportunities for reference to Wilde, and he is conspicuous by his absence. From the late 1930s onwards, the journal began a regular feature on the Dublin theatre – but the focus was always on contemporary works, so there were scant references to any playwright from before this period. There seems to have been a very definite shift of emphasis when the journal was relaunched as *Ireland of the Welcomes* in 1952 – with literature, music, festivals and other cultural activities coming to the fore. In *Irish Travel* in September 1928 an essay appears by F.P. Carey called 'Historical Houses in the Irish Capital':

> Among the memories of the Merrion Square houses the most arresting is perhaps that of No. 1, the birthplace of Oscar Wilde. It is, of course, sufficiently known that this extraordinary and unfortunate genius was born here; but public reference seldom takes account of the other interesting associations of the house. Sir William Wilde, father of the author of 'The Ballad of Reading Jail', was the actual tenant. He was one of the most eminent physicians of his day, a man who had put the record of a generation of medical research to his credit, and who had written extensively upon topics important to his profession. As well as this, he was a man of infinite culture, who took a practical interest in the intellectual movements of the age, a fact which, coupled with the taste and enthusiasm to the same end of his gifted wife – who was no other than the gifted poetess who charmed the readers of 'The Nation' from above the pseudonym 'Speranza' – this house became to Dublin exactly as the 'sun-teoi' had become to any of the centres of ancient Greece.[30]

Thus is Wilde elided in an account of his parents, contained and muted. Not all literary sources ignored Wilde, but it is significant that he is the focus of attention for Protestant Irish writers. In 1941, on the occasion of the eighty-fifth birthday of Bernard Shaw, the playwright Denis Johnston, Gate playwright and friend of Mícheál mac Líammóir, interviewed Shaw and included these musings on the different fates of the two Anglo-Irish playwrights.

> For all his iconoclasm, Shaw never seems to have done a really foolish thing in the whole of his life … Oscar Wilde ruined and disgraced himself at the very height of his powers, with an arrogance that can only have been deliberate and that disastrous plunge would seem at first sight to symbolise the truism that bad brilliant boys get what is coming to them and clever good ones get the first prizes. But I sometimes wonder whether Father Time has not still another joker up his

sleeve. We are beginning to realise that Wilde's disaster was really his apotheosis and gave a meaning to all his life. It will be interesting to see who lives longest – the foolish genius who died first or the clever genius who was always smart enough to keep out of mischief.[31]

Johnston was prophetic. Wilde became much more the revered figure of the two in Ireland after Shaw's death and into the twenty-first century. Later in the 1940s Wilde's name was evoked in the Irish Dáil in a debate on prison reform.[32]

In considering Johnston's account of Wilde in 1941, it is worth recording the ways in which Irish society dealt with the question of homosexuality at this time. The banning of Kate O'Brien's novel *The Land of Spices* in 1942 was a revealing moment about the language around homosexuality at this time. Kate O'Brien had already fallen foul of the Irish censor with her 1936 novel *Mary Lavelle*, where one Irish woman declares her erotic interest in another, which led to a banning. Again and again in her writings, O'Brien was unsettling her readers with her imaginative interest in the homoerotic. In her 1937 travel book, *Farewell Spain*, she wrote of the painter El Greco in this way: 'He is said to have been homosexual, but that suggestion can be of little use to us in considering his work. More mighty than he have been touched with that peculiarity but the residue of all emotional experience tends in spirits large enough to be at last of natural and universal value, whatever the personal accidents of its accretion.'[33] However, O'Brien never publically identified herself as lesbian. The lively debate over the representation of male homosexuality in *The Land of Spices* began in 1941 with a review by the Irish poet Austin Clarke, where he praised the novel for its autobiographical qualities and for the integrity of her representation of the spiritual life: 'In religious subjects, we have been dominated for years by the English convert mentality and have developed a self-conscious feeling of inferiority. But as writers, we have one considerable advantage over the converts. We have not to despise or disparage our earliest impressions in childhood.'[34] Austin Clarke's one criticism of the novel centred on a reference to the homosexuality of one character, the married man and exiled scholar Henry Archer: 'There seems to me one artistic flaw in this book, the nature of the shock which drove Helen Archer, the beautiful, intelligent young English girl into a Continental Order in a mood of agonized revulsion. It is an outwards shock, purely pathological and mentioned in a single, euphemistic sentence. A more personal experience would have given more scope for analysis and brought us nearer the girlhood of Helen Archer'.[35] Unease with the topic is also clear in the *Irish Independent* review titled 'A Masterpiece Spoiled', where the reviewer admired the book but felt that 'one could with charitable tolerance overlook some irritating passages. To use the word "loutish" in reference to a priest, and put into the Bishop's mouth words about education and the Irish language which are little better than gibberish, might be forgiven. But there is one single sentence in the book so repulsive that the book should not be left where it would fall into the hands of the very young people.'[36] The offending sentence was a description of a sexual moment between two men: 'she saw her father and Etienne in the embrace of love,' and this led to the banning of *The Land of Spices*. (It was published without difficulty in America that June.) The banning led to a public outcry in Ireland, as it was felt that the Censorship Board had gone too far in labelling this novel as obscene. A sustained campaign of protest was begun by, amongst others, the novelist Sean O'Faolain. Writing in his literary journal, *The Bell*, O'Faolain expressed his outrage: 'The official notice declares this book to be banned in Eire because it is "in general tendency indecent". Clearly this is a lie.'[37] There followed a series of attacks on censorship in the pages of *The Bell*, with Shaw, O'Casey and others defending freedom of creative expression. Finally, in November 1942, the Anglo-Irish landowner, Senator Sir John Keane, tabled a motion in the Irish Senate criticising The Board of Censorship. He used the particular incident of the banning of *The Land of Spices* as the focus for his opposition. In the Senate debate, Sir John Keane spoke of *The Land of Spices* with great respect:

> I have read it carefully and I may not be a very good judge but I consider that its general motif is almost religious . . . As anyone who has read the book will agree, the Reverend Mother depicted in it is a most noble character. She goes into the convent and takes the veil because she discovers, to her great surprise, that her father is given to unnatural vice. How she makes this discovery is important. If references to unnatural vice ran frequently through the whole book, and was dwelt on persistently I could understand, possibly, the grounds for objection. But it is a single reference and it is commendably short . . . for that phrase and that phrase alone that book is censored. Where that book can be held to be in its general tendency indecent or in the words of the definition 'to incite to sexual immorality or unnatural vice or is likely in any similar manner to corrupt or deprave' I cannot see.[38]

This tolerant and measured view on homosexuality is striking and rare, but he was overruled. However, there was a slight amelioration in censorship laws as a result of these debates and, in 1945, the Irish government introduced a board of appeal and Kate O'Brien's novel was unbanned. This episode is significant in that it gives a sense of the atmosphere in which homosexuality was considered in Ireland, but the novel is important also for its Wildean undertones. Kate O'Brien never wrote directly about Wilde (she did give a radio talk on Speranza as part of a series on Irish women writers),[39] but it is worth noting that O'Brien's novel does draw on Wildean notions of the homosexual in that her central character, Henry Archer, has certain affinities with Dorian Gray, as a Paterian figure of aestheticism and a disciple of Greek literature and Hellenic ideals.[40]

In 1942, T.G. Wilson published his life of Sir William Wilde, *Victorian Doctor*, an attempt to regild a somewhat tarnished reputation, sometimes at the expense of his son: 'This is the story of a man who, like his son, had many facets. Like his son also, his achievement was great – in fact, I am not sure that when the final judgement is made, he will not be pronounced the greater man of the two.'[41] Wilson's account of Wilde senior is heavy on medical history, given Wilson's own medical background, but he does discount some of the myths around Speranza, including the notion that her cross-dressing of Wilde made him queer, adding that 'The story is also unpleasantly reminiscent of the case histories of other unfortunate perverts.'[42] What holds Wilson's account together is a profound homophobia under the guise of medical and scientific detachment, a homophobia that may have included a dislike for Speranza. He muses about Wilde that 'Had he lived fifty years later, would he have been punished so severely? Or would he, in his arrogance, still have drawn his fate upon himself?'[43] Wilson contrasts the wholesome heterosexual affairs of Sir William Wilde ('Unlike Oscar, his vices were natural, and therefore more readily forgiven')[44] with those of Oscar, but Speranza is not treated with such sympathy and understanding. Wilson takes seriously Shaw's diagnosis that she was suffering from gigantism and concludes:

> If we accept this explanation, it gives us some sympathy for those unfortunate beings, like Oscar, whose perverted impulses twist and destroy some lives. In Oscar's life, other factors may enter – heredity is, of course, one of them, for he was very much his mother's son . . . Speranza, some say, was a suppressed homosexualist. If this is true, all the more credit to her for, unlike her son, she had the pluck to suppress it.[45]

One of the most important Irish commentators and scholars on Wilde ventured his first publication on the subject of the Wilde trials in 1948. The Ulsterman Hartford Montgomery Hyde was, as a scholar, as important as Micheál mac Líammóir as an actor and dramatist in influencing popular perceptions of Wilde in Ireland and elsewhere, and always to the betterment of an understanding of Wilde. Born in 1907, his background was Belfast merchant class, while his secondary schooling was in England. His father James Hyde was a Unionist Belfast councillor, although his mother[46] came from a more liberal, home-rule, Protestant background. He attended Queen's University Belfast where he gained a first-class history degree, and then Magdalen College, Oxford, for his law degree. He was called to the bar in 1934. Married three times, he was enlightened, liberal and well informed as a campaigner for homosexual reform, with many gay friends, particularly at Oxford, although older than his fellow students. At Oxford he occupied Oscar Wilde's rooms and later Hyde shared a room in MI5 with Guy Burgess. His first employment was with the seventh Marquis of Londonderry. From 1935 to 1939, he was librarian and private secretary to the Marquis, hired specifically to research the family's papers and write its history. He was with the British army staff in the USA from 1942 to 1944, attached to the Supreme HQ Allied Expeditionary Force in 1944, and then seconded to the Allied Commission for Austria until 1945. After the war, he became assistant editor of the Law Reports and then legal adviser to the British Lion Film Corporation.

In 1948, just before the Wilde estate was due to come out of copyright, Hyde published *The Trials of Oscar Wilde*, a precursor of three more Wilde books.[47] *The Trials of Oscar Wilde*[48] provided a balanced, honest and unflinching account of the three Wilde trials, drawing on the memories of surviving participants in the case, like Lord Alfred Douglas, Max Beerbohm and the last living member of Wilde's legal team, Sir Travers Humphreys. Hyde also interviewed Wilde's friends Yeats, Quiller Couch and Richard Le Gallienne. The official court shorthand writers and compilers of the Central Criminal Court sessions papers for the Wilde trials declined to print the proceedings because of the nature of the testimony and so many misconceptions and prejudices remained about the exact nature of the legal proceedings. In a spirit of truthfulness, Hyde was determined to present a full account of the case but was dependent on his own interviews with surviving witnesses and also on Stuart Mason's 1912 study, *Oscar Wilde Three Times Tried*. Hyde's book, a measured yet honest account of Wilde's homosexuality and his same-sex activities with Douglas and others, was banned in Ireland in September 1948 and then unbanned on appeal in December 1948. Afterwards it was reprinted several times, becoming the standard work of reference on Wilde's experiences in court and doing much to ameliorate his reputation in Ireland. Hyde used much of this material in his subsequent writings on Wilde, and in 1954 he presided over the unveiling of a London County Council plaque to Oscar Wilde at his home in Tite Street in Chelsea. Hyde's political career in relation to homosexuality is relevant to his writings on Wilde and also his progressive views on homosexuality. Hyde had planned a parliamentary career since the 1930s, and in 1950 North Belfast selected him as its Unionist MP. In his nine years in Westminster, he was a tireless advocate of reform on punitive measures against gay men in the UK. Hyde's earliest gay-related parliamentary intervention was a question tabled on police agent provocateurs after the acquittal in 1954 of Weng Kee Sam, a young Singaporean. He and another man, Frederick Beauchamp, who committed suicide before the trial, had been charged with gross indecency at Gloucester Road tube station. Sam later successfully sued the British Transport Police for £1,600 for malicious prosecution. The Home Office strenuously denied Hyde's suggestion of provocateurism when police carried out such 'distasteful duties', which were said to be 'essential to the preservation of public order and decency'.[49]

Hyde also debated the question of the authenticity of Roger Casement's 'homosexual' diaries in the Commons on 3 May 1956, when the junior minister William (now Lord) Deedes declined to depart 'from the [government's] policy of silence'.[50] In July 1959 Hyde called for the Home Office to admit that the diaries existed and to allow the public to see them. After the Wolfenden Committee published its report in favour of reform of the punitive homosexual laws on 21 May 1958, Hyde came second in a Commons ballot for notices of motion, and announced he would call attention to the report in three weeks. On 13 June, Hyde proposed that the House take note of the report of the Departmental Committee on Homosexual Offences and Prostitution. This courageous moment was to be Hyde's political undoing. In November 1958, when the government relented and allowed a debate, Hyde contributed a half-hour speech which was wide-ranging and thoughtful, and covered both aspects of the report. He concluded by demanding equality for the homosexual and the prostitute. The final government speaker, David Renton, spoke to decline the Wolfenden proposal, and decriminalisation was now shelved for a decade. In an interview with *The Irish Times* in 1985, Hyde recalled his loss of his Unionist seat and believed that it was as a direct result of his support for homosexual law reform.

> But when it came to the Wolfenden Report on the law relating to homosexual offences which I strenuously supported – in fact, Lord Boothby and I really started the whole thing and started the Wolfenden Committee – the caucus (of the Northern Irish Unionist Party) said 'we cannot have our member condoning unnatural vice'. That was it. That really finished me.[51]

Thus Hyde's reselection as MP was not ratified by his own party in 1959 and the Unionist Party lost its one respected voice at Westminster and abroad. Hyde's political undoing were his parliamentary interventions and outspoken views on the decriminalisation of homosexuality. (Eventually the 1967 England and Wales Sexual Offences Act was extended to Northern Ireland in October 1982, as a result of the ruling on Jeffrey Dudgeon's 1981 European Court of Human Rights case.)

After losing his seat, Hyde became Professor of History and Political Science at the University of the Punjab in Lahore in 1959 for two years, taking the opportunity to conduct research on Ulstermen who had worked in the Simla Hills and elsewhere in India. He also published two articles in May 1965 in *The People*[52] to advance the cause of homosexual law reform. A classic radical establishment figure, Hyde worked up to his death on 10 August 1989, just short of his eighty-second birthday, and in the next chapter I shall be discussing his later works on Wilde.

In 1949 *The Irish Times* carried an essay called 'The Man who was Oscar', a review of a book called *The Paradox of Oscar Wilde* by George Woodcock, where the reviewer, identified as 'RBDF', suggested that Wilde's books may have been removed from Irish libraries.

> The newspapers, from time to time, reveal the existence of librarians who remove from their shelves books which have given pleasure to everyone for years, because they feel that the writer has fallen from grace and it was inevitable that Wilde should be a prime sufferer from this kind of stupidity. On the other hand, the urge to defend Wilde has produced much foolish eulogy.[53]

The reviewer goes on to present a familiar, if regressive, notion of homosexuality as arrested sexual development and of bisexuality as a universal sexual identity. 'He was a man whose emotional life was in the same respects halted at a stage through which, as the psychiatrists will tell us, humanity in general passes. In a more enlightened age, he might have found treatment and a cure.'[54]

After the Second World War and by the early 1950s, Ireland was experiencing the call of social change, or if not change, then the demand for change. After the war, the old dichotomy between dissent at home and exile in Europe began to break down. New social and economic influences from a post-war literary culture began to suggest the possibility of change for Irish writing. Terence Brown writes that

> There were various signs that a new Ireland, an Ireland less concerned with its own national identity, less antagonistic to outside influence, less obsessively absorbed with its own problems to the exclusion of wide issues, was, however embryonically in the making . . . 'We must look outward again or die, if only of boredom', wrote the poet and critic Anthony Cronin in *The Bell* in 1953.[55]

Accounts of Wilde, his literary estate now being out of copyright, slowly began to change within Irish popular culture at a time when, as Tom Garvin writes, 'In the late 1950s, an almost panicky decision was finally made to modernise'.[56] Connected to this was a very gradual shift in perceptions about homosexuality. In the UK, as Matt Cook suggests, 'After World War II, homosexuality had come to be seen as a social problem and personal tragedy, and not as integral to any discourse of rights or a broader left-wing political agenda.'[57]

However, Irish opinion remained, for the time being, conservative. In 1953, Patrick Ryan published his biography *The Wildes of Merrion Square* with an English publisher, Staples Press, in 1953 and opens his account of Wilde's parentage with a celebrated moment in the nationalist iconography around Speranza, the trial of Charles Gavin Duffy in 1849 and the intervention of a 'lady', unnamed, who tried to claim authorship of the revolutionary article 'Jacta Alea Est'. In his account, Ryan idealises Sir William as a great scholar and Speranza as a great Irish patriot but is frank about their other relationships before they married. In a now-familiar fashion, Speranza is approved of for her patriotism but blamed for effeminising her son (without any direct biographical proof): 'In her emotional and eccentric way, she would insist on treating Oscar as if he were a baby girl, and she obstinately battled against facts.'[58] Ryan develops this idea of Lady Wilde's influence on her son's sexuality when he writes about her 'dualism': 'Much has been written on the supposed dualism in the character of Oscar Wilde. Lady Wilde herself had early been impressed by what she called the dualism in the lives of the German philosophers.'[59] Her intellectual dualism becomes translated into Wilde's sexual duplicity. Ryan continues: 'The narrative of the downfall of Oscar Wilde has its distasteful elements and there is always something disturbing in excessive punishment',[60] but adds that 'Psychologically Wilde was always a latent homosexual, but like many such, it required a combination of circumstances to confirm the perversion.'[61]

Ryan's account of Wilde's sexuality is hostile in the extreme, but this didn't prevent the book from being banned in July 1953, as most books on Wilde seem to have been at this time. It was then unbanned in October 1953. There is no record of Wilde's own texts being banned in Ireland at this time, only studies of his works or biographies. Ryan recounts that 'Wilde did actually boast in a witty after-dinner speech that he had adopted many poses for the benefit of his art and that now he might find it necessary to pose as a homosexual',[62] and deplores the fact that 'The persistence which prompted Wilde to engineer his own destruction has excited interest, as has the fact that he was sincerely convinced that homosexual practices were not criminal and were even ethically exculpable . . . A martyr he may have been, according to a certain view, but few causes are advanced by martyrdom.'[63] Ryan concludes that

> There is little doubt that from the year 'Eighty-seven' or 'Eighty-eight' Wilde experienced a sort of mental exaltation or unbalance which corresponds with the time he became a practising pederast. This in turn coincides with his best period as a creative artist. Modern psychological investigation has been concerned with the connection between the creative urge and the homosexual, but that is a matter which we cannot pursue here.[64]

The book was reviewed in *The Irish Times* by Cathal O'Shannon, who commended its 'brightness' and 'readability' but who found many factual mistakes. 'More surprising still, in a writer of Mr Ryan's experience, a number of historical howlers occur.'[175] Letters were exchanged between the writer and the reviewer in *The Irish Times* about these 'historical howlers' but to no clear conclusion.

The most hostile of all the Irish accounts of Wilde came from the Belfast playwright St John Ervine (1883–1971). Born in east Belfast and working as an insurance clerk, Ervine became a member of the Fabian Society, where he became friendly with Shaw and others and began a career as a dramatist. His first play was staged in the Abbey Theatre in 1911 and he became manager of the Abbey Theatre in 1915. His disillusionment with the Abbey and with what would become the new Irish state started with his opposition to the Easter Rising and as a result he joined the Dublin Fusiliers, saw some fighting in France where he was seriously wounded and lost a leg. After the war, Ervine moved to Devon, becoming a successful West End playwright in the later 1920s and then moving on to write a number of social realist novels set in his native east Belfast. His success as a biographer is reflected in the range of his subjects: Shaw, Carson, Craig (a staunch believer and defender of the northern state), and a study of intense admiration and devotion on C.S. Parnell.

Ervine begins his study of Wilde promisingly enough with the statement that 'Oscar Wilde . . . has been dead long enough for an opinion of him and his works to be formed without prejudice',[66] but goes on to produce the most prejudiced and antagonistic account of Wilde in twentieth-century Irish writing: 'Reviled unreasonably, he was stupidly applauded.'[67] Both Speranza and William Wilde come in for attack in the most hostile and malicious terms: 'Neither of the Wildes had any sanctity to dispense. Their second son Oscar was damned on the day that he was born and would have done better to have died in childhood as his sister Isola, who followed him, did.'[68] Sir William is characterised as 'undersized and ugly, he had the features of a ferret',[69] while his wife is dismissed in these terms: 'Lady Wilde was an affected and ridiculous woman.'[70] The Wilde parents, according to Ervine, contributed nothing to national life, culture and literature in Ireland, but it is the subject of Wilde's sexuality that moves him to lengthy quotations from the Old Testament:

> There is perhaps, too much tendency today to make light of sodomy, too great a tendency to condemn harshly without attempting to understand those who were most ferocious in their denunciation of Wilde's offences . . . Fornication is natural sin, sodomy is not . . . Sodomy is a denial of life, a cult of sterility . . . It is our will to live, and live abundantly, which turns our mind against the pederast.[71]

All through this, Ervine seems to forget that Wilde had children.

Ervine attacks Wilde's genealogy of gay art, used as a defence during his trials, arguing robustly for the heterosexuality of Christ and Shakespeare but willing to concede that Da Vinci might have been sexually suspect. He judges Wilde as more culpable sexually, because he chose to move from his married life towards gay relationships: 'He was deliberately sodomistic. He not only practised the vice, but believed that it should be practised. He denied that it was a vice.'[72] Ervine quotes Shaw and Douglas to illustrate his point that Wilde refused to excuse or deny his homosexuality and was unrepentant about his sin. Ervine's prose at times becomes bizarre in his anger against Wilde – at one point, worked up against Wilde's sexual sins, Ervine mentions 'mincing stable-boys',[73] an incongruous mix of homophobic clichés. Unsurprisingly, Constance is dealt with sympathetically, the only member of the Wilde family to escape the vitriolic attack: 'It was not much fun to be Mrs Oscar Wilde.'[74]

Ervine intersperses his sustained attack on Wilde with biblical quotations against sodomy, and statistics on the increase of homosexual prosecutions in the UK in the late 1940s, and returns again and again to blame Speranza for Wilde's education in sin. Ervine's antagonism towards the Irish Republic is evident: 'Showing off is a common fault in Ireland. Wilde had it in an extraordinary degree.'[75] This deeply felt anger and dislike of the southern Irish state becomes intertwined with his homophobic loathing of Wilde when he lists all the Irish writers who refused to live in Ireland. 'All these authors from the Eirean area calculated very cunningly how they should get on, and decided that England was the place for them. They shook the Irish dust off their shoes and departed for the alien shore, where they performed the tricks the English expect from the Irish.'[76] Curiously, Ervine reverses the accepted and comforting belief expressed by other Irish writers on Wilde that Oxford, and thus England, corrupted him sexually. 'Some men at Trinity have suffered from sodomy and the vast majority of Oxford graduates in all ages have been free of it . . . If sodomistic tendencies were started in him at all in this period, they are more likely to have been caused by his tour with Dr John Pentland Mahaffy in Italy and Greece in 1877, although proof that they were cannot be found either in his acts or his words.'[77]

Despite the initial blame attached to Trinity College Dublin, Ervine is uncompromising in his blame and attack on Robert Ross for introducing Wilde to same-sex activities: 'Ross, a sly, intriguing, suave and timorous little fellow, possessive as a maiden aunt, will, we may surmise, receive a dusty answer when he comes smirking into the courts of God with that claim to immortality on his lips. What hell will be deep enough and dark enough to hold him when he is violently hurled from heaven for corrupting and debauching a brilliant mind?'[78] (So now Ervine momentarily allows that Wilde has a brilliant mind!)

Despite his hatred of Wilde, Ross and other openly gay men, Ervine evinces a inexplicable liking and admiration for Alfred Douglas, calling him 'This superb and dazzling descendant of all the Douglases',[79] asserting that Douglas had paid for some of the trial expenses, despite Wilde's denial in *De Profundis*. In relation to *De Profundis*, Ervine takes some pains to discredit Wilde's story of standing on the platform at Clapham Junction on his way to Reading Gaol and being jeered at and mocked by a hostile crowd at the train station. Ervine asserts that there would not have been enough people around at that time of day in a small suburban railway junction to form such a mob and is anxious to brand Wilde a fantasist and take away any sense that he could have been an object of pathos.

He concludes that 'The Wilde of the last two years was a Wilde in an advanced state of degeneracy. He was now a rabid hunter of small boys and simple-minded conscripts.'[80] 'Wilde came into the world with a small talent and made little of it. That was the sin committed by Oscar Wilde. It was the sin against the Holy Ghost.'[81] Why was he so opposed to Wilde and sympathetic to Douglas? His perspective is perhaps that of the working-class Ulster Protestant Unionist, at odds with the southern state but loyal to empire and to the notion of aristocracy.

Early in 1954, the centenary of Wilde's birth, mac Líammóir wrote to the Irish newspapers suggesting that members of the public might subscribe to the placing of a suitable tablet on the façade of the house in which Wilde had been born – 21 Westland Row, Dublin. A similar tablet was being placed on Wilde's London home in Chelsea, paid for by Greater London Corporation. In *The Irish Times* of July 1954, in 'An Irishman's Diary', Pro Quid Nunc, an article called 'Second Thoughts' made the point that:

Now that the centenary of his birth has come around, the plain people of Ireland seem to have decided that for all his short comings, Oscar Wilde was not the worst of them. Indeed, although there is a certain air of veiled embarrassment about our celebrations, the conviction seems to be growing that in his own odd way, he was quite a credit to Dark Rosaleen . . . We in Ireland are charmingly tolerant of weaknesses of the flesh and I believe that we might be quite prepared to overlook Oscar's perverse shortcomings if only he had done anything that would enable us to palm him off as a patriot . . . But Wilde was resolutely a West Briton and by no stretch of the imagination can he be converted into a patriot malgré lui.[82]

In his 'Cruskeen Lawn' column in *The Irish Times* on 11 September 1954, the novelist Brian O'Nolan, writing under the name of Myles na Gopaleen, took up the argument:

Oscar Wilde was not an Irishman, except by the statistical accident of birthplace. He had become completely déraciné and living in England before he was twenty. Not one shred of his literary work even suggests an Irish inflection . . . If plaques and statues are to be the order as before, why pick Wilde? Surely there should be precedence in the order of such public gestures. Does [Hilton] Edwards suggest that Wilde is the foremost of Dublin's unremembered men?[83]

In response, T. Nisbet of Harry Street, Dublin, wrote to the editor of *The Irish Times* on Tuesday 14 September 1954 to say, 'According to Myles, Oscar Wilde was only Irish by virtue of geographical accident and was not in the habit of boasting about his origin. Nevertheless I am all for this polite body snatching idea of a plaque . . . For the Irish and proud-of-it type I suggest a stork making a forced landing. In any case, let Erin remember.'[84]

In his biography of mac Líammóir and Hilton Edwards, Christopher Fitz-Simon mentions that 'There was no local authority scheme at that time to pay for the erection of such memorials and he [mac Líammóir] soon found himself secretary and honorary treasurer of a self-appointed committee . . . The cost was only £62.12.6d but the subscriptions, even at £1, were slow to come in. Fáilte Ireland, the Irish tourist board, refused to be associated with the project, as did leading commercial organisations. It was believed that there was still a slur over Wilde's name, although half a century had passed since his trial and imprisonment in London . . . The plaque was unveiled by the playwright Lennox Robinson, who received a tomato on his shirt front for his pains.'[85] Lennox Robinson unveiled the plaque on the house in Westland Row, Dublin, where Wilde was born, on 16 October 1954. Robinson, the son of a Church of Ireland clergyman, a dramatist and director of the Abbey

Theatre, was part of that tradition that sought to reclaim Wilde the Irishman, despite the doubts and objections. The *Evening Herald* reported, front page, on 16 October that 'Dr Robinson said he wanted emphatically to emphasise Wilde's Irishness'.[86]

On 19 October *The Irish Times* published Micheál mac Líammóir's BBC broadcast tribute to Wilde in full, with many familiar notes of appropriation struck.

> We have raised a plaque in marble on the walls of the Dublin house where, a hundred years ago, Oscar Wilde was born on October the sixteenth. I and a few friends have planned to do this because all of us in Ireland who admire his work and believe him to have been a man of significance wish him to be remembered as a portion of that contribution that Ireland, through a series of historical events, has inevitably made to literature in the English language and to the tradition of the English theatre. We wish to remind our countrymen that Wilde was an Irishman . . . Wilde an Irishman? Was he not tribe less and nation less . . . True Wilde's Irishry was of the old-fashioned school. He was courageous in the old Irish way, he was proud, indolent, reckless, easily led, companionable, heedless, hard-drinking, and gregarious and swaggering . . . Those of us in Ireland who revere the best of his work and from whom his personality has won an almost personal affection are inclined to grudge the heaping of his gifts onto the rich lap of England. We forget too, in our regret, that his mother's fervent if somewhat spasmodic nationalism did not manifest itself in her son. That had he stayed in Ireland, had he undertaken the work of Yeats in stemming the drainage of blood from Ireland's artistic life, Ireland would have most likely never have noticed him. England gave him brilliant recognition and she followed it with a sentence that to one of his temperament was a sentence of death. Ireland, after one amused and friendly glance, would have asked him who in the name of goodness he thought he was and allowed him to do little more than talk and dream and drink himself into a condition of virtuous apathy. But Ireland would have given him a glorious funeral.[87]

Later Robinson published his own speech on Wilde in 1956 in his collection of memoirs, *I Sometimes Think*, and his main motivation is to make an acceptable Irish Wilde. At the beginning of his speech, Robinson stresses that, 'I want to begin my discourse by emphasising his Irishness'.[88] Here was another Irish Protestant voice making a claim for Wilde's nationalism, with no mention at all of his sexuality, his misdemeanours, just the pathos of prison and a reiteration of his Irish nationalist credentials.

Wilde's mother came from County Wexford, her family were of the ascendancy class, but, as a young girl from the country walking through St Stephen's Green, the crowd was so dense that she could not pass. It was a funeral. 'Whose?' 'Thomas Davis's.' 'I've never heard of him.' She went home and read him; she read other works of the Young Irelanders. In a few years time she was 'Speranza of the Nation' . . . From Trinity he went to Oxford and from that time onwards it might be thought that his connection with Ireland had been entirely severed. But paternal, maternal, school and college influences are not quickly eradicated and when at the age of twenty-seven he went to America on a lecture tour, he said 'As regards the men of '48 I look on their work with particular reverence and love, for I was indeed trained by my mother to love and reverence them as a Catholic child is the saints of the calendar, and I have seen so many of them also. The earliest hero of my childhood was Smith O'Brien, whom I remember so well, tall and stately, with the dignity of one who had fought for a noble idea and the sadness of one who had failed – no perhaps I should not use the word failed – such failures are at least often grander than a thousand victories.' He spoke with love and awe of Thomas Davis, 'the greatest of them all'. That is why there are Gaelic words on the plaque.[89]

Like Yeats and Shaw, Robinson constructs the very public failure of Wilde's life as something heroic in the Irish nationalist mode, and includes only one reference to his private life, a mention that is safe and heterosexual: 'Wit is so often cruel, but Wilde seems to have been the kindest of men and I cannot discover that he ever did a rough or unfeeling thing. He adored his children . . . sang songs in Gaelic to his little boys, songs he had learned from his father.'[90]

The Irish newspapers covered the unveiling of both London and Dublin plaques. In the *Sunday Independent*, it was reported that 'Mr Hilton Edwards read a message from Mr mac Líammóir who is acting in London in which he said: "We would have the passer-by remember that although it was England who gave him his fame and his infamy it was Ireland who gave him those qualities that made him the most memorable tragic comedian of his age."'[91] *The Irish Times* radio reviewer G.A. Olden on 21 October commented on all the Wilde plays, lectures and talks on BBC and Radio Éireann and asked,

Is genius perhaps too strong a word for this man of rare and brilliant accomplishment . . . who fell foul of the Criminal Law Amendment Act . . . The speaker ended by asking us to consider that suffering and punishment at length brought wisdom and understanding to Oscar Wilde but was that seriously the case? Certainly suffering promoted the chastened spirit out of which came *De Profundis* and

The Ballad, but surely Wilde's repentance was as much a literary attitude as his pagan intransigence? The pathetic history of his last years hardly accords with this picture of the Wilde lamb redeemed.[92]

In the *Evening Herald* of 14 October, a letter to the editor was published from John Cusack, Herbert Road, headed 'To Oscar Wilde – Why?' and asked 'It is intended to erect a plaque on a house in Dublin to Mr Oscar Wilde. Why? Can you or any of your readers enlighten me? If it were intended to erect a plaque to commemorate Speranza, I could understand and would favour the proposal.'[93] A P.J. McL replied on 27 October with this: 'In reply to John Cusack, I would like to state the following; Oscar Wilde was born in 1854 and died in 1900. He was a student at Magdalen College, Oxford. In 1878, he won the Newdigate prize for his poem, "Ravenna" . . . I hope this information will be of some use to Mr Cusack.'[94] John Cusack replied on 22 October querying the date of Wilde's birth and asking if the committee had advanced the date by two years.

The September–October 1955 issue of *Ireland of the Welcomes*, the official journal of Fógra Fáilte, the national tourist publicity organisation for Ireland, carried an article by Seán O Faoláin entitled 'Writers' Conquest' about the 'imperial conquest' by Irish writers of the English language. Wilde is the first name mentioned, but his 'Irishness' is questioned:

> A number of Irishmen who wrote magnificently in English were reabsorbed, in turn, back into English literature – Wilde, for example, and Shaw, and even George Moore: but nobody will ever think of calling Yeats or Joyce or Synge English writers, or Seán O'Casey, or Liam O'Flaherty, or James Stephens. These latter typify the literature which we call Anglo-Irish because it is written in English. But it is, in practice, Irish literature.[95]

Interestingly, Brendan Behan is one of those twentieth-century Irish writers on whom Wilde's influence can be most directly ascertained, particularly in his short story 'After the Wake' (1950) and his 1954 play *The Quare Fella*. In a time of official homophobia, Wilde was, for these writers, a covert sign within this hidden tradition, a symbol of sexual dissidence. At first glance, it is an unlikely influence. Behan was born in 1923 in a working-class tenement in the north side of Dublin's inner city to a profoundly Republican family – his uncle wrote the national anthem of the new Irish state. Behan, who trained as a house painter, joined the IRA as a teenager and, as a result was sentenced to spending time in Borstal in England. Behan found in works like *De Profundis* and *The Ballad of Reading Gaol* a heady mixture of the homoerotic, of Irish defiance of British justice, of letters written in English gaols and of powerful court-room speeches, and his work reflects these influences. While in Borstal in England between 1939 and 1941, his biographer records the first encounter of the teenage Irish Republican with the emblematic and decadent name of his fellow Irishman.

> In the library, he met a fey young man of about nineteen, who wore a rose coloured silk tie and smoked through a cigarette holder. This young man was reading a copy of Frank Harris' *Oscar Wilde*. He explained to Brendan exactly why Wilde had been jailed. This revelation was meant to be disturbing but Brendan responded sharply that every tinker has his own way of dancing.[96]

Although Behan later married, his biographer tells us that 'When among friends, he often used to boast drunkenly of his Herod complex, or preference for young boys.'[97] Later, Behan's 1954 prison play *The Quare Fella*, centred on the imminent execution of a wife murderer, is a work which pays direct homage to the influence of Wilde. As a biographer, Michael O'Sullivan recounts: 'It was inevitable that reviewers in Ireland would make a comparison with Wilde's *The Ballad of Reading Gaol*. In the *Evening Press*, Gabriel Fallon found it more profoundly moving and deeply religious than Wilde's great prison letter.'[98]

Wilde was a talisman for Behan, particularly during his time in Paris in the late 1940s. One example was this 1949 poem, originally written in Irish, which celebrates Wilde on his deathbed in Paris:

> The young prince of sin
> A withered churl
>
> . . .
>
> Good man yourself there, Oscar,
> Every way you had it.[99]

Behan's fellow drinker and sometime adversary Patrick Kavanagh did not share this idealised view of Wilde the rebel. Writing in the *Irish Farmers' Journal* in 1960, Kavanagh judged and dismissed Wilde in these terms: 'Wilde, a wonderful wit, was not among the world's greatest. When misfortune overtook him, he caved in. The great men such as Socrates or Dante never accepted the values of their enemies . . . Wilde's genius was his wit; he was a poor poet.'[100]

In 1960 two British films about Wilde were released, *The Trials of Oscar Wilde* and *Oscar Wilde*, and both were immediately banned by the Irish film censor, much to the annoyance of Irish film critics. Around this time, Sir Shane Leslie, a cousin of Winston Churchill, wrote of Wilde's conversion to Catholicism, playing up 'the interesting traces of Catholic dispositions at the beginning as well as at the end of Oscar Wilde's ill-starred public life'.[101] Leslie traces Wilde's sincere interest in Catholicism and the many attempts to undo or unsettle his attraction to Rome. Throughout, Leslie highlights the Catholics who helped Wilde on his way, yet denies his homosexuality.

> Publicly he dethrones Respectability and crowned Beauty in its place. Let it be noted that he bowed to feminine beauty. He accepted the normal passions of the Garden of Eden, and far from decadent, married one of the fair, who made him a happy home. The trials have been too often told. Not only was Oscar punished but his innocent family as well.[102]

It is worth noting that in *Ireland of the Welcomes* intermittent mention is made of Wilde's name.[103] First of all, there was more of a literary emphasis in the issues produced in the 1950s, whereas, from maybe the mid-1960s onwards, there is a tendency to plan issues around historical anniversaries (beginning obviously with 1966 and the Easter Rising). From then on, there were a number of issues dedicated entirely to one theme. From perhaps the late 1970s onwards, the subject matter of articles became more and more diverse, and thus references to literary figures became less prominent. Issues were set aside to individual counties or festivals or events (such as the Pope or an American president's visit to Ireland). Wilde was never the subject of an issue (unlike Joyce or Synge) or of even an article in his own right. Just about every other prominent Irish literary figure was the subject of an article at some point, and these tended to repeat every five or so years (Joyce, Yeats, Swift, Goldsmith, Synge).

The editors were especially fond of articles talking about these figures and their surrounding: for example, 'Joyce's Dublin' or 'Yeats's Country'. There seems to be a problem associating Wilde with a geographic space that is distinctly Irish. It was not until 1976 that there is an article about Wilde, or, more accurately, the Wildes. The piece was written to commemorate the death of his father and highlight the achievements of the parents. For example, the May–June issue in 1953 carries a picture of Oscar Wilde's home on the corner of Merrion Square – listed with landmarks linked to Joyce, Synge and Goldsmith. Also, there are pictures of Swift, Shaw and Richard Brinsley Sheridan.

The September–October issue in 1959 carries 'Dubliners All' by H.L. Morrow, an article about the dearth of commemorative plaques in Dublin, which gives brief biographies of twelve 'great men' who should be immortalised on plaques – Edmund Burke, Roger Casement, James Joyce, Thomas Moore, Edmund O'Donovan, Padraig Pearse, G. Bernard

Shaw, Richard Brinsley Sheridan, Charles Villiers Stanford, J.M. Synge, Oscar Wilde and W.B. Yeats. In the essay on Wilde, Morrow notes that 'as a result of a misguided libel action against the Marquis of Queensberry, followed by imprisonment, [Wilde] spent his last days in Paris in neglect and poverty'.[104] Also in the May–June issue in 1961, in 'From the Bookshelf' (a regular feature on newly released books of general Irish interest), there is a review of the book *Oscar Wilde* by Vyvyan Holland (the reviewer is not named).

> Oscar Wilde was one of the most exciting personalities of his genera-
> tion. Already a legendary figure as an undergraduate at Oxford, he
> rapidly became the most successful playwright and the most cele-
> brated conversationalist and wit in the English-speaking world. His
> downfall and descent from being the darling of the salons to an object
> of the most vicious calumny was not only a remarkable cause célèbre
> but also a pitiful tragedy.[105]

Ireland was to undergo great change, even a cultural revolution, in the 1960s. In the words of David Cairns and Shaun Richards, 'The change in political leadership in 1959 from the austere, aged figure of Eamon de Valera to his successor Sean Lemass, Fianna Fáil taoiseach from 1959 to 1966 was followed by what contemporaries regarded as an intellectual revolution.'[106] Likewise the name of Oscar Wilde was to be transformed within Ireland due to the work of one man, Micheál mac Líammóir.

4. The mac Líammóir revolution: 1960–1970

Wilde was the invisible but by no means inaudible bond who made the road I was facing less chilly . . . That magician whose name was my secret for ever more (Micheál mac Líammóir, *An Oscar of no Importance*)[1]

In this chapter, I argue that the most important figure for the transformation of Wilde's reputation in Ireland was actor and dramatist Micheál mac Líammóir (1899–1978). Mac Líammóir was born Alfred Willmore in London in 1899 but gaelicised his name and reinvented himself as an Irishman. In the late 1920s he moved to Dublin, setting up his Gate Theatre with his life partner, the director Hilton Edwards, and quickly establishing himself as a central figure in Irish theatrical life. His widely performed play *The Importance of Being Oscar* (1960) presented an acceptable version of Wilde, his life and his writings, for a wide audience in Ireland and elsewhere. The many performances of this popular show were crucial for the process of cultural acceptance and rehabilitation of Wilde's name in Ireland, but the openly gay mac Líammóir and Edwards achieved this transformation, this revolution, by heterosexualising Wilde. Taking their cue from *De Profundis*, they reconstructed Wilde as helpless victim, sidestepping any details of his sexual downfall and finding tragedy and pathos in his fate. Mac Líammóir performed his 'safe' version of Wilde's life in theatres, schools and all over Ireland from 1960 to 1970 and thus facilitated a sea change in Irish attitudes towards Wilde. In his 1968 memoir of the show, published under the title *An Oscar of no Importance*, mac Líammóir permitted himself some frank speculation on Wilde's sexuality:

> Yet how fortunate he was. Not merely because without the catastrophe he would be remembered as the author of a handful of underrated and little read books and plays, but, by the very nature of the scandal that ripped the last rags of decency from him, posthumous writers can discuss him and his work with complete frankness, as no other homosexual artist, leading a discreet and reasonable private life, can even in our time be discussed.[2]

As a result of mac Líammóir's Wilde show, new versions of Wilde's sexuality could be accommodated and presented in mainstream social discourse in Ireland, permitting a contemporary reclaiming of Wilde the gay Irishman.

For nearly fifty years the invented figure Micheál mac Líammóir, actor, dramatist, painter, designer, Gaelic scholar, theatre manager (and 'Corkman'), dominated Irish theatre with his programme of experimental, poetic and continental dramas. In his own Gate Theatre, founded in 1928 with Edwards, mac Líammóir provided a less insular, more cosmopolitan, alternative to the state-subsidised Abbey Theatre and maintained a counterbalance to the peasant dramas and rustic comedies of establishment theatre with a programme of Wilde, Coward, Ibsen, Pirandello, Eugene O'Neill, Anouilh and others. In the partners' own words, the aim of the Gate Theatre was to 'have in Dublin a permanent company presenting dramas of all nationalities, to experiment in new methods of production and design and to widen the sphere of Irish activity in the theatre'.[3] Terence Brown, in his *Ireland: A Social and Cultural History*, considers their contribution to Irish cultural life thus: 'Only the work of a few individual poets, novelists and artists of the nineteen-twenties gave any hint that the dismal obscurity that Shaw feared might not envelop the country.' Brown goes on to cite 'mac Líammóir's presenting European drama at his Gate Theatre and his Irish language theatre in Galway.'[4]

Just as significant, mac Líammóir was also that most unique of figures within post-independence Ireland: the openly homosexual public figure. In a state where homosexual acts were criminalised until 1993 and the homoerotic was censored and expunged from all official literary and cultural discourse, mac Líammóir and Edwards survived, and even flourished, as Ireland's only visible gay couple. A strikingly handsome man in his youth, mac Líammóir maintained his looks into old age, Dorian-like, a familiar and popular figure on the streets of Dublin. This was no mean achievement within a culture where in 1941 Kate O'Brien, mac Líammóir's friend and contemporary, had an entire novel banned for one homoerotic sentence. When mac Líammóir died in 1978, the president of Ireland attended his funeral, as did the taoiseach and several government ministers, while Edwards was openly deferred to and sympathised with as chief mourner.

Yet 'Micheál mac Líammóir', supposedly Cork-born Irish actor and writer, never actually existed. As I have stated, it was a name and a personal history conjured up by London-born actor Alfred Willmore when he left England for Ireland in 1917. Alfred Willmore, born in Kensal Green in London in 1899, had no Irish connections whatsoever. He had been a success as a child actor, working with Sir Herbert Beerbohm Tree amongst others, and then had attended the Slade School of Fine Art.

However, just before graduating from the Slade, Willmore abandoned his studies and went travelling. In the short term, Willmore was fleeing Britain because of conscription and possibly also because of the attentions of an older, wealthy lover. As his biographer Christopher Fitz-Simon argues, 'There is no reason to doubt that as Alfred's seventeenth birthday approached he would have been dreading the arrival of his call-up papers.'[5] More acutely, he was also seeking, in the aftermath of the Wilde trials, an acceptable persona within which to be both homosexual and, at the same time, visible. Alan Sinfield, in his study *The Wilde Century*, contends that a particular and threatening concept of 'the homosexual' came from Wilde's public persona and was implicated in his disgrace: 'The dominant twentieth-century queer identity, I will argue, has been constructed in this kind of process, mainly out of elements that came together at the Wilde trials, effeminacy, leisure, idleness, immorality, luxury, decadence and aestheticism.'[6]

To escape association with this newly forged deviant sexual role, Willmore reversed Wilde's own journey of self-consummation. He left London for Dublin, initially to act with his brother-in-law Anew McMaster, embracing Celticism and remaking himself as an Irishman. Thus he found in the role of the Irish mystic artist a denial of the taint of Wildeian aestheticism and decadence. Throughout his life, in his various autobiographical writings, mac Líammóir was to tell and retell the narrative of this youthful decision to leave London and to adopt Dublin as his theatrical base (each retelling involving a creative reordering of the narrative to accommodate and justify his assumed mask or persona): 'Here is London, a huge impersonal web of shadow and movement and like a vast motherly hen, the night broods and waits . . . Home again to Ireland, to a new Ireland, maybe.'[7]

In essence, Alfred Willmore reconstructed himself as the neo-Celtic thespian mac Líammóir, a disciple of Yeats and of the Celtic Twilight, because the Yeatsian mask would enable Willmore to dissent and separate himself from British masculinist heterosexuality. In other words, with the shadow of Wilde and the Wilde trials making the homoerotic suspect and questionable in Britain, the Yeatsian mode of artistic being offered a more acceptable role for the sexually ambiguous actor and dramatist, and so Willmore reinvented himself, taking on the mantle of the Celtic Revival. However, to maintain this fictive persona, his autobiographies turn on a series of evasions and screenings, obscuring his English origins and veiling his sexual identity, delicately treading a balance between artistic licence and downright 'fiction', i.e. invention. In this chapter I select a few of his dramatic and autobiographical writings – *An Oscar of no Importance* (1968) and *Enter a Goldfish* (1977), both volumes of autobiography, and two of his plays, *The Importance of Being Oscar* (1963) and *Prelude in Kasbek Street* (1973) – to assess Wilde's shadow in his imagination. I will argue that, once established as a neo-Yeatsian, mac Líammóir discovered that this artistic persona became less and less tenable. Therefore his theatrical work, especially during the 1940s and 1950s, became increasingly arid and uninspired. It is my contention that the emblematic figure of Wilde licensed the actor to bring his dissident sexuality more and more to the fore. In my view, his final play, *Prelude in Kasbek Street*, and his last volume of autobiography, *Enter a Goldfish*, are vitalised by a new centrality of the homoerotic. Mac Líammóir made Wilde acceptable in Ireland again.

By his own account, mac Líammóir's meeting with Edwards in June 1927, in Enniscorthy, Co. Wexford, was a pivotal moment in the construction of his fictive persona. Private and public roles and national and sexual identities were resolved and anchored for mac Líammóir in his partnership with Edwards. (Alfred Willmore's decision to remake himself as the Corkman Micheál mac Líammóir may have had something to do with the fact that he and Edwards, out of work and penniless, moved on directly from Wexford to Cork, formulating plans for a new Irish theatre in the southern capital.) In a professional sense, the actor/designer found the ideal director, with Edwards's exacting production values checking and harnessing mac Líammóir's lyricism and self-dramatisation. The two were to live together for fifty years. However, Edwards provided the perfect Saxon foil against which mac Líammóir could define his Irishness, his literary reincarnation as poet of the Celtic Twilight.

In all his autobiographical writings, mac Líammóir plays this game again and again, the native-born son explaining the essentially inexplicable nature of Ireland and the Celtic imagination to the interrogating Englishman: 'We would pass by thatched whitewashed houses that looked rose-coloured in the moonlight, and by brown running streams whose voices seemed like the rushing of the world through space and, at times, I would try to explain Ireland to him.'[8] He wrote elsewhere: 'How, indeed, could we foresee, Ireland or I, that he, with the Englishman's uncanny knack for turning tables, would make both of us work far harder than we had bargained.'[9] (In actuality, it seems from biographical evidence that Edwards had more real Irish ancestry than Willmore.) Added to this is a denial of any English connections. Mac Líammóir's rejection of London is seen as a racial necessity, the striving of the Celtic soul to free itself from the stranglehold of metropolitan culture.

> I had been brought to London an infant in holland overall, and as a stage child in a sailor suit, I had loved it and then, adolescent, I had hated it again and fought to escape and here I was in a pinstripe suit

in 1935, a self-made alien, breathing the air that might have been my own. And I wondered was I right to choose the narrow Irish road and I know now that the choice was inevitable. Even my partner, had he wished, could not have changed that in me, though in all else I was putty in his hands. For good or for evil, the Irish way was part of me; there really had been no choice at all.[10]

Mac Líammóir's theatrical career had three distinct phases: the Yeatsian phase – the 1930s and 1940s; an interlude of stagnation – the 1950s; and finally the Wildean phase – the 1960s and 1970s. W.B. Yeats afforded him a secure artistic mode within which to become an aesthete without the taint of Wildean sexuality: '. . . turning Wilde's monstrous orchid into a wet bulrush.'[11] Mac Líammóir claims Yeats as an emblematic muse figure: 'I had read Yeats' "Ireland and the Arts" for the first time at fourteen.'[12] At one point, Edwards rails jealously against the overweening influence Yeats has had on mac Líammóir: 'National Yeats was your god. He had shaped everything in your programme long before you met him.'[13] How precisely did mac Líammóir engage with Yeats as a mentor figure within his own theatrical activity? There is, undoubtedly, some manifestation of Yeatsian influence in his *Diarmuid and Grainne* (1935), an influence later acknowledged in his one-man show *I Must Be Talking to My Friends* and in his study *W.B. Yeats and His World* (1977), written with the poet Eavan Boland. However, in *All for Hecuba* there is no accounting for mac Líammóir's lack of contact with Yeats's own Abbey Theatre, or for the profoundly divergent programmes in these two Dublin theatres, or even for the fact that mac Líammóir, during Yeats's time at the Abbey, appeared in only two productions. His one recorded meeting with Yeats reflects something of the unease of their relationship: 'But I felt that he only half approved of me as an exponent of the Celtic Twilight, which in those days of self-conscious virility was at its lowest ebb, and I, in my heart, agreed with him. These were no times for echoing the vanished rhapsodies of the Nineties.'[14]

Towards the close of *All for Hecuba*, he writes of the death of Yeats and, referring to Ireland's artistic soul, asks the question: 'What new stamp would be pressed into the changing wax, softened again into shapelessness with the death of the poet?'[15] Mac Líammóir may have been talking about Ireland, but there is also a sense that Yeats proved an unsatisfactory and inadequate personal muse for mac Líammóir himself. Wilde was more relevant as a figure of an emblematic dissident. There was a clear sense that by the beginning of the 1950s the Gate had failed to sustain itself as an integrated and consistent force within Irish theatre. As Terence Brown comments: 'Neither [Gate and Abbey theatres] managed quite to create that sense of new awakening that had characterised the early years of the

Irish literary theatre.'[16] In *All for Hecuba*, mac Líammóir has Edwards attacking him for his obsession with his supposed Irishness, blaming their enforced residence in Dublin for a certain staleness in their work. In his pamphlet *Theatre in Ireland* (1950), he allows that 'a period of uncertainty, even perhaps of stagnation, in the Irish theatre and its literature may be at hand'.[17] By 1957, Edwards was urging mac Líammóir to leave Ireland, writing to him to ask 'whether it is worthwhile to give anything more to Ireland considering the prospects she has left us with after thirty years'.[18] Yeats dwindled as a source of inspiration for mac Líammóir because, ultimately, as a writer, he found Wilde to be a more direct source of personal revelation. One of the code terms for the homosexual in mac Líammóir's time was 'unspeakables of the Oscar Wilde sort',[19] as used by E.M. Forster in his novel *Maurice*. As his career progressed into the 1960s, he allowed the unspeakable Wilde to speak again at a time when attitudes towards homosexuality were changing.

H. Montgomery Hyde comments that, when the Wolfenden Report on homosexual offences and prostitution was published in England in 1957, 'it received a very largely favourable press and was welcomed by practically every organisation which had submitted evidence to it, as well as by leading spokesmen of most of the Christian denominations'.[20] In 1954, the centenary of Wilde's birth, mac Líammóir wrote to some of the Irish newspapers suggesting that members of the public might subscribe to the placing of a suitable tablet on the façade of the house in which Wilde had been born, at 21 Westland Row, Dublin. This interest in Wilde culminated in the one-man show, *The Importance of Being Oscar*. It was created by mac Líammóir and Edwards and then directed by Edwards, and was first performed on 15 September 1960 at the Curragh Barracks in County Kildare, for Irish army officers and their families. When it opened in Dublin in the Gaiety theatre, Christopher Fitz-Simon records that '*The Importance of Being Oscar* opened to a very warm response. All the reviews next day were more than favourable.'[21] In an article headed 'Three hours of triumph for mac Líammóir', the *Irish Press* reviewer commented that 'mac Líammóir painted Wilde's life with a gentle brush'.[22] In a thoughtful review in *The Irish Times*, the writer commented that 'this triumph belonged to two people, Oscar Wilde and Micheál mac Líammóir' although making the shrewd point that 'all of Wilde was not shown to us, that his sins were smoothed over by his regret'.[23] The *Irish Independent* applauded the humour and wit and made the point about the representation of Wilde that 'we began to see him in the round, have a fuller understanding of him and though there is much to deplore, the feeling in the end was one of compassion for the man and of a greater understanding of his many-sided genius'.[24] This success led to a series of American and European tours and, eventually, a television dramatisation. Another biographer, Micheál Ó hAohda, calls this time in their career the 'reingreencarnation'.[25] This led to a worldwide touring of the play and great financial success for the pair.

Given that the name of Wilde had been employed throughout the twentieth century as a shorthand code for homosexual identity, mac Líammóir's reading of Wilde in his one-man show *The Importance of Being Oscar* (1963) was very partial, shaped by a need to present an acceptable version of Wilde and of his fate. Contemporary lesbian and gay theorists have reclaimed Wilde as a powerfully disruptive figure, a sexual rebel and a social transgressor. However, in this version, mac Líammóir fixes on Wilde the tragic hero, not Wilde the rebel, Irish or otherwise. Edwards introduced the published text of the performance in the following terms: 'It shows him to have been aware, from the first, of the inevitability of his tragedy.'[26]

In his narrating within *The Importance of Being Oscar*, mac Líammóir chose to distance himself from Wilde, recounting his life and his writings rather than impersonating Wilde directly. This allowed him to construct a Wilde of his own making. Edwards and mac Líammóir took Wilde's fall from grace as their theme and saw that fall as consequent on his fatal glorification of the erotic: 'I did but touch the honey of romance / And must I lose a soul's inheritance?'[27] However, the honey of Wilde's romance in this version is predominantly heterosexual. Wilde's key act of transgression, his infatuation with Bosie, is referred to in one telling phrase: 'that tiger life'.[28] Setting a tone of world-weary despair and ennui, mac Líammóir keeps all his sexual referents strictly heterosexual. In the first half of the presentation, Wilde's passion for Lily Langtry and his love for Constance, his wife, are recounted. Indeed, the readings from *Salome* and *The Picture of Dorian Gray* concentrate on Herod's lust for Salome rather than on her eroticisation of Iokanaan's body, and on Dorian's murderous instincts rather than on Lord Henry's and Basil's love for Dorian's beauty. After these straight moments from Wilde's writings, mac Líammóir inserts a short interval. During the interval, Wilde's affair with Bosie, his 'tiger life' with London rent boys and the three trials are presumed to have taken place. In the second act, the play deals solely with Wilde's prison writings and the consequences of Wilde's sexual deviancy are rendered with pathos and melodrama. Wilde's dignity in prison and in exile, his composed yet passionate reproach to Bosie in *De Profundis* and the stark anguished compassion of *The Ballad of Reading Gaol* all serve to engender a sympathy with the erring outcast. His final fable, *The Doer of Good*, although dealing with lust and the despair of the erotic, is firmly heterosexual.

However, playing Wilde, or at least interpreting Wilde as predominantly straight, led to questions that mac Líammóir was not quite ready to answer. Joan Dean has researched the two North American tours of *The Importance of Being Oscar*, and her account of these various reviews reveals that there was a greater cultural difficulty with Wilde and with the hidden theme of his homosexuality in the United States than in Ireland. The first American performance of the show began in the Lyceum Theatre on Broadway on 14 March 1961 and led to a four-week season. American reviews, positive in many ways, were, at the same time, as blunt as they could be about the gay implications of the subject and of the production. The *New Yorker* commented that 'Despite Mr mac Líammóir's innumerable skills, his performance will of necessity appeal only to a fairly specialized audience.'[29] The *World Telegraph and Sun* believed that 'the show can only have a specialized appeal'.[30] As Joan Dean has written, 'Encoded was a bristling over of any mention, let alone, a sympathetic treatment of homosexuality. If it wasn't just a disease, it certainly was still a crime.'[31] Despite some hostility, *The Importance of Being Oscar* returned to the United States in October 1961 for an extended tour, where the First Lady, Jackie Kennedy, attended a performance of the play in Washington.

In *An Oscar of no Importance*, mac Líammóir recounts an incident during his later South African tour of the show when a woman journalist challenged him directly on the subject of Wilde's sexuality and, by implication, his own.

> 'You', began a small, plump, very firm-looking lady, gazing at me through her spectacles as though she would burrow into the depths of my soul, 'are going to act as Oscar Wilde?' 'Not act as him: I try to interpret him.' 'Well then, I would be interested to know, as you have chosen him rather than another writer, what is your own attitude to the question of male homosexuality?' I gazed back at her in a prolonged moment of silence, as of deep cool waters whose apparent tranquillity might be haunted by many sharks . . . Did she mean among cattle or human beings? But I never received an answer.[32]

Neither, in point of fact, does the reader – yet! It is worth pointing out that neither man felt confident enough to come out at this stage in their career and, in fact, no mainstream Irish writers were to define themselves as openly lesbian or gay until 1993. Mac Líammóir and Edwards felt sufficiently confident as to the climate of public opinion on Wilde to present the show all over the world and, indeed, the 1960s were an important decade for the republishing of Wilde's texts and his rehabilitation as an artist. Although emboldened by the success of the one-man show, there is evidence that they were still hesitant about highlighting the homoerotic in their theatrical work. Indeed, it was not until mac Líammóir was in the final decade of his life that he wrote his most directly 'gay' play. Changes in British law and in censorship in the theatre and the experience of working on Wilde all had a cumulative effect on mac Líammóir's writings on the homoerotic. Sinfield writes that

> It is no accident, then, that the English legislation governing both theatre and homosexuality was reformed when the Labour Party was elected with a big majority on a modernizing platform in 1966 . . . The Wolfenden proposals were enacted in 1967 and theatre censorship was abolished in 1968 . . . It enabled many gay men and lesbians to refuse the discreet spirit of the law and, with varying degrees of flamboyance, to come out.[33]

Thus mac Líammóir's memoir, *An Oscar of no Importance*, is a revealing account of the way in which the one-man show on Wilde brought him face to face with the nature of Wilde's sexuality and with the implications for his own creativity.

In many ways, *An Oscar of no Importance* is, as the title suggests, a mirror text for *The Importance of Being Oscar*. All the evasions of the stage play are dealt with directly in the memoir. In considering the relationship of the play to the memoir, it seems as if mac Líammóir found the public arena of theatre, as yet, an unsafe place in which to speculate on Wilde's sexual nature. Where the play concentrates on the normative aspects of Wilde's life and writings, the memoir displays no such reticence. It opens with surprising directness, relating a childhood incident where he quizzed his embarrassed father as to the exact nature of Wilde's unspeakable crime, eventually provoking this outburst: "'What was wrong with Oscar Wilde?' 'He turned young men into women.'"[34] In the course of the memoir mac Líammóir explores his professional and personal bonds with Wilde, 'that magician whose name was my secret for evermore'.[35] He even allows himself to theorise on Wilde's sexual identity. He claims a more direct kinship with Wilde than in his previous writings: 'Wilde was the invisible but by no means inaudible bond who made the road I was facing less chilly.'[36]

In relating the process by which he devised the one-man show with Edwards, mac Líammóir incorporates a candid account of Wilde's sexuality into the memoir, but adopts a tone of objectivity throughout. His attitude to Wilde is one of worldly understanding: 'All right, so he was "so" [the twenties slang word for the contemporary word 'queer'].'[37] His account of Wilde's sexual history is forthright and clear-sighted.

> He had been initiated into homosexual practices, as the legend has asserted, by Robert Ross himself, and difficult as it may be for the

mind of today wholeheartedly to believe that this was in truth his very first experiment, there is a great deal of evidence to show that he had been in fact passionately in love with his own wife, and had been strongly attracted throughout his earlier manhood by many other women. It was likely too that it was the experience with Ross that decided him to accept himself for the future completely as a pederast and to lose all his previous interest in the opposite sex. Robert Ross stated that the affair began in 1886, the same year that English law adopted the statute that nine years later was to cause Wilde's arrest and imprisonment: one could be forgiven for wondering could it have been the very same day that Queen Victoria signed the statute? At the very same moment, it may be, when Wilde decided to respond to the enamoured Ross, so closely the web seems woven about him.[38]

Much can be deduced from the above account of mac Líammóir's own concept of homosexual attraction, a concept that also informs his later writings, including *Enter a Goldfish* and *Prelude in Kasbek Street*. Same-sex desire, as he presents it, is a matter of choice and he is anxious to frame the homoerotic within the context of heterosexuality. Mac Líammóir makes a distinction – and a necessary duality – between the 'born invert' and the 'convert', a distinction that surfaces again in his later writings. He places Wilde within the second category and speculates as to whether or not Wilde's very public 'tiger life' was, in fact, a reaction to his earlier heterosexuality: 'Is it the enthusiasm of the convert? This, in Wilde's case, was perversely heightened by a violent and very personal sense of sin, which, in the born invert, is absent.'[39] Mac Líammóir finds Wilde's blatant disregard for potential notoriety disturbing and seeks to explain the almost suicidal disregard that Wilde had for public opinion and for the legal consequences of his sexual transgressions. Side by side with this unease at Wilde's supreme confidence is a need to find such openness commendable.

> Yet how fortunate he was. Not merely because without the catas-
> trophe he would be remembered as the author of a handful of
> underrated and little-read books and plays, but because, by the very
> nature of the scandal that ripped the last rags of decency from him,
> posthumous writers can discuss him and his work with complete
> frankness, as no other homosexual artist, leading a discreet and rea-
> sonable private life, can, even in our time, be discussed. Unless they
> pass into a vast immortality, of course, like Socrates or Shakespeare
> or Sappho or Michelangelo or Leonardo. It does not matter very
> much what we say of them: like the sun they are so undeniable, and
> like the sun they were born so long ago. But with later and lesser
> artists, the case is different. The life they had so wisely and so pru-
> dently hidden from the world succeeds at once in hiding their

shameful secret from the world and in forever preventing their chroniclers from giving a full-length portrait. [40]

It seems as if he almost envies Wilde his open, unambiguous sexual identity, openness not as available to mac Líammóir 'even in our time', or so he hints. In this memoir he is prepared to discuss Wilde's 'sin' frankly and openly, but always as the impartial, uninvolved outsider, rarely allowing his own connection with Wilde to surface, and keeping his own life apart. As narrator, he presents himself as judge and unbiased arbiter of moral conduct, fair-minded, rational, methodical, and stripping away the prejudices against Wilde's aberrant sexual life, and finding in his disaster a kind of achievement:

> Did I believe him to have been a bad man who, like so many bad men, provides an interesting study in abnormality? I do not believe him to be a bad man. His only 'badness' in my eyes is that he failed to fulfil the destiny imposed upon him by potentialities unguessed at even by those who idolised him at the hour of his triumph, perhaps especially by these. He himself was aware of them. Spiritually, if one may be allowed an outmoded, outworn term, he was a failure. Yet failure itself, bowed down with broken dreams, is essentially a part of him.[41]

Yet, here and there, mac Líammóir lets his own personal stake in Wilde and in Wilde's sexual nature become apparent. At one point, discussing the difficulties of staging and playing *The Importance of Being Oscar* and the tension brought to his relationship with Edwards, he confesses: 'Suddenly I saw what *The Importance of Being Oscar* threatened to do to our lives in the theatre. "And our personal lives, too", he [Hilton] added when I spoke of this.'[42]

Mac Líammóir's last stage play, produced in 1973, is also his most candidly 'out' play and one where he finally permits himself to discuss the nature of same-sex desire on stage. The question must be asked: Why, after forty years of a highly visible partnership, did mac Líammóir and Edwards wait so long to stage a play like this? Their biographer, Christopher Fitz-Simon, offers the opinion that 'Had it been produced thirty years before, it would have caused uproar . . . Both Edwards and mac Líammóir genuinely believed they were taking a risk.'[43] Even with the changing climate of public opinion on the subject of same-sex relationships and the change of legislation in Britain in 1967, he approached his subject with circumspection. As a result, *Prelude in Kasbek Street* is, in parts, an equivocal play. Edwards, who directed the play, noted this and wrote: 'There is a tendency to fear the theme and to dance off into comedy which is inclined to make the comedy obtrusive.'[44] However much mac Líammóir 'feared' the theme, it is significant that, at the end of his career, he was finally prepared to present the homoerotic on stage after his 'reingreencarnation' with Wilde.

For *Prelude in Kasbek Street* mac Líammóir chooses a contemporary setting, the 1970s, and a cosmopolitan milieu, Paris, to dramatise issues of sexual and national identity. The protagonist, Serge, a celebrated ballet dancer, is also a displaced and reconstituted national subject, having started life as John Joseph Cassidy. Within this acquired pseudo-Russian identity, Serge exists both as artist and also as sexually different. The play opens with a violent row between two gay lovers, Serge and his 'companion' Jean-Louis, but this row is in French, thereby screening the vehement passion of their relationship, now at the point of break-up. Although it is mentioned that the lovers have had separate bedrooms and the word 'companion' is used by Serge's housekeeper, Mrs Baty, to describe Jean-Louis, mac Líammóir leaves us in no doubt as to Serge's emotional needs and interests. This is effected through the overt use of symbol, signalling Serge's quest for love, in the title of the play.

The name Kasbek is a reference to the 1913 ballet *Thamar*, presented by Diaghilev's company in London. Mac Líammóir might have seen the ballet as a teenager in London, and here he parallels Serge's life with the historical story of Tamara, Queen of Georgia. Tamara, a tyrant of medieval Georgia, lived and ruled from her castle at the Kasbek Pass, and legend has it that she lured handsome young men into her castle, made love to them, and then had them killed (a historical fabrication because the real Tamara was a shrewd and successful warrior queen). Serge associates himself with this man-eating queen when he relates the legend to his housekeeper Mrs Baty, thus explaining his attraction for 'normal', i.e. straight, men as being symptomatic of a self-destructive sexual destiny. Serge is the devouring Tamara, always involved with the wrong sort of man, the kind attracted by his fame and flattered by his attention, but always returning to women as the preferred choice of sexual partner. Mac Líammóir is vague as to the true nature of the parallel between Serge and Tamara, but what is clear is that he is using the play to present his own concept of same-sex desire. Mac Líammóir replicates his earlier notion of necessary opposition between Celt and Saxon in this drama of sexual politics. This opposition has the effect of creating in Serge, the man who is 'so' or 'queer', a fated propensity to be attracted towards 'normal' men exclusively. This potentially destructive sexual dynamic is the driving force behind the play, and the course of the action follows Serge's attempts to escape this dynamic.

The defence and justification of homosexual desire is provided not by Serge, but by his friend and compatriot Maggie (Madame Gonzales). When Jean-Louis leaves him, Serge fears loneliness and death. He turns to his friend Maggie for consolation. Maggie attempts to comfort him by providing a broader perspective on his sexual destiny: 'Isn't your misery partly because of the world's attitude to your sort of person? People always laugh at what they cannot understand . . . They think your sort of person unnatural.'[45]

Maggie continues in her defence of the homoerotic, much as Wilde did, by evoking Shakespeare and Michelangelo as exemplary gay men and Serge admonishes 'the world for turning the whole thing into tart for tart's sake'.[46] Invigorated by Maggie's consciousness raising, Serge gains a sense of empowerment: 'If my sort of person is represented in a book or movie as high or low camp, something both comic and con-temptible, people will lap it up. If it is pornographic, it's acceptable permissiveness. But if it's given one shred of dignity or reality, God help us!'[47] In his lament for the lost Jean-Louis, Serge rationalises his own compulsive need for love with someone 'normal', someone inartistic. Maggie concurs, comparing him directly to Tamara, the man-eater: 'You need a life companion, what is known as a normal man.'[48] In the dia-logue between Serge and the worldly, sympathetic Maggie, the playwright goes to great lengths to defend and to exonerate same-sex desire and at one point nearly trips himself up when he has Maggie say: 'You're not the cheap promiscuous sort like so many of your tribe, God help them, sure what else can they do.'[49]

Mac Líammóir, now too old to play the lead, appeared in the play as Gonzales, the husband of Maggie (a role notable only for its being written completely in Spanish). Nevertheless, Serge is mac Líammóir's alter ego, the cosmopolitan aesthete, the tragic diva in search of true love. Much of mac Líammóir's final writing turns on this imaginative device. He resurrects the youthful experiences of the child actor and 1920s' artist, but revitalises these experiences with a new frankness, a willingness to speak the name of forbidden love because of Wilde.

His final volume of memoirs, written in the year before his death, was published by Thames & Hudson in July 1977 and received a warm recep-tion from the Irish and British press. However, some reviewers expressed puzzlement at his use of the third-person narrative. Sheridan Morley in *The Times* wondered if it could be called a novel, 'partly, because some of the details have already been outlined in the rich, if confused, tapestry of mac Líammóir's other writings: more probably, I suspect because it details one or two homosexual and other encounters which even at this late stage the author is not prepared to document more fully'.[50] Another reviewer, the playwright Denis Johnston, also queried this form: 'This per-sistent vein of anonymity has the peculiar effect of encouraging the reader into a deeper suspicion of the facts than of the fiction.'[51] These questions about the veracity of his last memoirs are difficult to understand when one considers the writer's lifelong habit of self-invention. *Enter a Goldfish* is simply the final act in this continual process of self-generated drama, a fictive rendering of a life already completely fictionalised. Ultimately, the new point of departure in this final version, in comparison with all the previous autobiographies, is a new willingness to focus on the homo-erotic. He is remaking his life, but this time he is empowered by his encounters with Wilde. *Enter a Goldfish*, otherwise a tiresome rendering down of mac Líammóir's early life into some sort of family sitcom, is invigorated by a latent frankness in sexual matters. He closes *Enter a Goldfish* with the meeting between Martin Weldon and his future partner, Linden Evans (Hilton Edwards, thinly disguised), referring to them as 'the Couple' and prophesying complete personal and professional happiness for them both.

More importantly, the ending of the memoir indicated the fact that mac Líammóir had reached a point in his writings when public and private discourse could be accommodated. It meant that the homoerotic, ironically that which characterised him most directly in Ireland, could now be articulated in his writings. For mac Líammóir himself as a writer, the lifelong taboo on the love that dare not speak its name had eventually been broken, and the unspeakable was finally made to speak through his writings on Wilde. For public perceptions of Wilde in Ireland, mac Líammóir had effected a revolution.

5. Reinventing Wilde
the Irishman:
1960–2000

> The 1960s were to be a time of both radical change and apparent radical change. (Dermot Keogh)[1]

Ireland experienced radical economic, legal and social change during the last half of the twentieth century and into the twenty-first century and so the name of Oscar Wilde was refashioned to suggest or even invent a more inclusive sense of Irishness. In an unproblematic way, his name was gradually re-appropriated by contemporary writers and critics, and within cultural discourse as a symbol of modernity and new-found tolerance, but with many of the old stereotypes still embedded. In the wake of Micheál mac Líammóir's normalising and popularisation of Wilde's work, critical attention from Irish scholars led to this reclaiming of his Irishness; this was also paralleled with public interest in Wilde, in terms of lectures, summer schools, statues and exhibitions, during the 1990s and into the new century. Firstly, from the 1980s onwards, there was an increasing scholarly discussion around the Irishness of Wilde and his writings, including him within a broader tradition of reclaimed Protestant Irishmen and women like Swift, Shaw, Beckett and Bowen. This led to academic studies establishing Irish influences and patterns beneath the surface of his London society comedies and his prose. For the rest of this chapter, I want to consider the scholarly and critical versions of Wilde produced during this time of change and his altering cultural status within Irish public life, and then, in the next chapters, I will discuss the various imaginative representatives of Wilde's life and sexuality into the twenty-first century. Later in this chapter I discuss the biographical writings of H. Montgomery Hyde, and Davis Coakley's 1994 biographical study *Oscar Wilde: The Importance of Being Irish*, as well as Declan Kiberd's 1995 *Inventing Ireland*, where links between Wilde's national identity and his sexual 'outsiderness' were being made in a new and more direct way. During this time, Richard Pine's 1995 *The Thief of Reason* stands out as the first full-length study linking Wilde's sexuality and his Irishness. Then a collection of essays, *Wilde the Irishman* (1998), edited by Jerusha McCormack, extended the range of critical perspectives on Wilde's Irishness, offering solid scholarly reflections upon the ramifications of Wilde's racial identity and suggesting his place within contemporary theories of Irish writing.

However, mac Líammóir's work took place in the face of stringent attitudes towards homosexuality and this was to continue until the early 1990s. Diarmaid Ferriter details the background in legal and political terms when he argues that 'homosexuality was not something that was regularly discussed or acknowledged publically in the Republic in the 1960s'.[2] He goes on to quote statistics to show that, between 1962 and 1972, there were 455 convictions of men for indecency with males and gross indecency, 342 of whom were over the age of 21 and would not have been prosecuted in Britain. While Wilde (like Burke, Swift, Shaw and Bowen, amongst other Irish protestant writers) was being re-appropriated as part of growing critical interest in Irish writing as post-colonial, side by side normative Irish sexual identities were also under pressure for reevaluation. J.J. Lee writes that 'The preoccupations with sex, the virtual equation of immorality with sexual immorality, conveniently diverted attention from less remunerative tenets of Christian doctrine . . . Not until the 1970s did the idea take root, and then only precariously, that public morality could concern anything other than the sexual lives of public men.'[3] This meant a gradual alteration in ideas around homosexuality and, eventually, around the idea of Wilde as both homosexual and also Irish. Wilde's shadow was now to become a mirror, a reflection of social and legal change, and a signifier for modernisation.

It is significant, I think, that all the important Irish studies, biographies and imaginative re-creations that attempt to reread and reclaim Wilde's life come after decriminalisation of male homosexuality in June 1993. This change in the Irish law in 1993 came as the result of a twenty-year campaign for reform. The Irish Gay Rights Movement was founded in Dublin in 1974, five years after the Stonewall Riots in New York had galvanised worldwide politicisation for lesbians and gay men. The campaign for the decriminalisation of male homosexuality in Ireland (already abolished in the UK since 1967) came as part of a broader call for liberalisation on censorship and on repressive legal control around sexuality in Ireland in the 1970s and the 1980s. The battle around decriminalisation was a difficult one, like many of the social debates and battles in Ireland at that time. In the words of Tom Garvin, 'In the 1980s, Catholic forces in the form of the priests, bishops and knights fought aggressive, successful and often unscrupulous battles on the issues of divorce and abortion. These were Pyrrhic victories which possibly merely rendered the emergent liberal consensus far more angry and even implacably anti-Catholic than it ever need have been.'[4]

One such battle began when a university lecturer in English literature at Wilde's alma mater, Trinity College Dublin, David Norris, took a case in the Irish courts against the Irish government in 1980, arguing that the criminalisation of homosexuality in Ireland was an infringement of his civil rights as an Irish citizen. The High Court in Dublin found that the anti-gay laws were not unconstitutional. Diarmaid Ferriter writes:

> As Norris recalled, the difficulty was not just a legal one, but a barrier in terms of popular and political prejudice. When the High Court case was dismissed in 1980, he appealed to the Supreme Court, which also rejected his case, the Chief Justice, Tom O'Higgins, asserting that 'the deliberate practice of homosexuality is morally wrong, that it is damaging both to the health of individuals and the public and finally that it is potentially harmful to the institution of marriage. I can find no inconsistency with the Constitution in the laws that make such conduct criminal' . . . Barry Desmond recalled that the advice available to the government from counsel was that the AIDS argument should be used if it was a factor in the Government's thinking on the desirability of retaining present laws.[5]

To further the fight against legalised homophobia, in 1983 the campaign group GLEN (Gay and Lesbian Equality Now) was founded and intensified the pressure for law reform. The emergence of a number of national lesbian and gay organisations by the late 1980s meant that right-wing pressure groups in Ireland responded with a counter-campaign. Despite the best efforts of these right-wing activists, decriminalisation eventually took place after lobbying led the European Court of Human Rights to rule that Ireland's anti-gay laws contravened the European Convention on Human Rights of 1988. In response to this ruling, on 24 June 1993 Dáil Éireann passed a Bill decriminalising homosexuality. David Norris, now a senator in the Irish Seanad, wrote in *The Irish Times* on 25 June 1993: 'When next week, this Bill is passed by Seanad Éireann and sent to the President for signature I will, for the first time in my life, feel that I am at last a full and equal citizen in my own country.'[6]

One of the results of this legal action was a real sense of empowerment and acceptance for Irish lesbian and gay people. From the 1990s and onwards into the new century, openly gay Irish writers, musicians and public figures moved Irish gay identities from the margins into the mainstream as a visible cultural presence. As Fintan O'Toole suggests in writing about Ireland in the new millennium: 'Already feminist, gay, working class and diaspora readings and reconstructions have done much to suggest the possibilities of a set of alternative pasts that can do in criticism what creative writers have been doing in prose, poetry and drama. Even only as a vacuum, the past will remain a force in Irish writing.'[7] Part of that past was Oscar Wilde and now he was to be modernised, made contemporary with Celtic-Tiger Ireland, a citizen of a

queer Irish nation and both rebel and sexual hero. But to what extent did
the New Ireland replicate the versions of Wilde already seen in the
earlier decades of the century?

Productions of his plays during the period 1970 to 2004 numbered
around 130 in mainstream Irish theatres. From the mid-1960s onwards,
biographies of Wilde continued to appear in Ireland and, taking their cue
from mac Líammóir, an increasingly sympathetic portrait of the victim
Wilde emerged, a figure of tragic suffering. In the various studies of
Wilde during this period, the figures of Wilde, his mother, Bosie and
Constance all were reinvented and reconsidered.

In 1963, Hyde published his *Oscar Wilde: The Aftermath*, a study dedicated to those in favour of penal reform and written in the wake of
Hyde's own parliamentary career and his efforts to introduce more
enlightened legislative attitudes towards homosexuality. In his preface,
Hyde tells of his efforts in 1954 to read the original 1895 Wilde prosecution papers and files, which were now supposed to be legally available for
public scrutiny for the first time. Hyde was blocked by the notoriously
homophobic British Home Secretary Maxwell Fyfe, who refused him
permission, saying they would pain living people, despite the fact that
Wilde's son Vyvyan Holland supported Hyde in his efforts to read the
primary evidence. A later Home Secretary was to allow Hyde full access
to the files and these papers became the basis of his book.

In addition, Hyde was the first member of the public allowed to see
the original and unedited *De Profundis*, on 1 January 1960, when the
British Library was legally entitled to open the sealed manuscript. Hyde
supported prison reform and also gay legislation reform in the UK and
Northern Ireland, and he was using this new evidence of Wilde's time in
prison to paint a picture of unnecessary and disproportionate suffering:
'This is the story of Wilde's imprisonment and the effect which his punishment had on him . . . I feel it deserves to be remembered.'[8] Hyde
characterises Wilde's term in Reading Gaol as marked by 'terrible
severity'[9] and details the physical deprivations, hunger, hard work and
daily cruelty of his incarceration. In a characteristically measured and
well-written account, Hyde creates a picture of Wilde as acceptably pen-
itent and even heroic: 'The lesson which Wilde set himself to learn in
prison was that of humility.'[10]

This is in no sense a work of hagiography. Hyde is fair-minded and
uncompromising in his presentation of Wilde's shortcomings and gives
full details of Wilde's various financial dealings and also of the fallout
with Constance Wilde's solicitors over the control of her money. Hyde
also includes new evidence from the men who worked in Reading Gaol

and attests to Wilde's popularity and humanitarianism in relation to wardens and fellow prisoners. He also includes, from the Irish point of view, an interesting fact about the petition that Frank Harris tried to organise, in an effort to have Wilde released from prison a few months early. Many eminent writers refused to sign, with some angry at being approached, although one Irishman did volunteer: 'In the end, Harris only secured one signature, and that was entirely voluntary and unsolicited. It came from Professor R.Y. Tyrell, Regis Professor of Greek at Trinity College Dublin, who remembered Wilde in college and through Harris sent him a friendly message in prison – "Confusion take all their English Puritanism" – he said as he wrote his name underneath the petition.'[11] Hyde concludes with an account of Wilde's release from prison and the publication of *The Ballad of Reading Gaol*. Later Hyde was to continue his enlightened engagement with Wilde when he wrote a fair-minded, balanced account of Bosie's life, as well as a groundbreaking history of homosexual scandal, *The Other Love*.

The literary editor of *The Irish Times*, Terence de Vere White, was another important Irish source on Wilde. Born in 1912 and literary editor of *The Irish Times* from 1961 until 1977, de Vere White was also a friend of mac Líammóir and Hilton Edwards and was associated with the Gate Theatre. De Vere White was the author of twelve novels and also produced biographies of Isaac Butt, Thomas Moore, George Egerton and Kevin O'Higgins, and a study called *The Anglo-Irish* in 1972 with a chapter on Wilde. In his introduction to his 1967 biography *The Parents of Oscar Wilde*, he states that his aim was to restore respect to Sir William and Speranza, because they had, in his opinion, 'acquired something of the inevitability and pathos of the routine vaudeville act'.[12] De Vere White does indeed evince some initial respect for Speranza, 'to her, he [Oscar Wilde] owed most of his qualities, for good and all',[13] but he does see the whole Wilde family as tainted by inordinate sentimentality and a hint of decadence: 'Whatever strain was in the Wilde family that led to sexual disorder and disaster?'[14] De Vere White, in his treatment of Wilde, is, on the whole, sensible, with something of an air of worldly scepticism, but once or twice he falls back on a note of disdain, referring to Speranza as 'something of a pantomime queen'.[15] He does take seriously the claim that, at the Charles Gavan Duffy trial, she tried to speak up and take responsibility for her treasonous writings in *The Nation*, and he explicitly challenges St John Ervine's dismissal of her role in court on that day. De Vere White thus links Speranza's nationalist stance in court that day with her subsequent influence on Oscar, and connects it with Yeats's later story that she urged her son to stand his ground after losing the case against Queensberry. He deals sensibly with her 'culpability' in relation to his homosexuality and the commonly held supposition that her childhood cross-dressing of Wilde turned him gay, making the point that this was: 'An unlikely supposition as Oscar was three years old in 1857, an early age then for a starkly masculine rig-out to be prescribed for boys so as to ensure the development of heterosexual tendencies later on.'[16]

De Vere White makes the point that the Catholic church in Glencree has no record of the supposed Catholic baptisms of Willie and Oscar in 1862, as told by the American priest Fox, and also that Shaw is the only source for the idea that Speranza was suffering from gigantism. In his account of the trials, de Vere White retells Yeats's story about her urging Oscar to stay, and comments: 'Who can deny that Yeats was right, or that Speranza's instinct, as always at great moments, was noble?', but goes on to say, 'It is doubtful if his mother played much part in his decisions. He lived in a sort of euphoric trance . . . What she thought about it, nobody knows. She is said to have professed to the last her belief in his innocence.'[17] De Vere White gives her more dignity and, at the same time, less Irish nationalistic importance in relation to Wilde.

De Vere White returned to Wilde in his lively and anecdotal history *The Anglo-Irish*, published in 1972, with a very short but shrewd chapter placing him within this Irish Protestant world. He opens with the revealing assertion that, 'When Yeats called his roll of honour, he left out the name of Wilde. But not today, although so far as land and horse-owning is concerned he fails to qualify as an Anglo-Irishman.'[18] Unlike his earlier study, de Vere White here is flippant and dismissive – 'Oscar played down his Irishness in London'[19] – and debunks the idea that Speranza saw Thomas Davis's funeral passing her Leeson Street home, thereby becoming converted to the cause of Irish Republicanism. This is a lively pen portrait but lacking the substance of his earlier study.

Hyde's *The Other Love* was published in 1970, a well-researched and sympathetic account of famous (or notorious) same-sex scandals and trials in the UK from the sixteenth century onwards. Hyde's consistent commitment to reform and tolerance is evident in this work, a wide-ranging account of homosexuality from William the Conqueror through to Wilde, the Cleveland Street scandal and the Cambridge spies. (Interestingly Hyde focuses on a number of Anglo-Irish homosexual scandals, including the trial of the Earl of Castlehaven, the Dublin Castle scandal and the theft of the Irish Crown jewels.) Hyde's opening chapter is a frank examination of modes of sexual activity, statistics, and the prevalence of misconceptions about homosexuals and their dress codes and social encoding. As a work of original historical research into a submerged sexual subculture, it is outstanding and remains a key reference source for contemporary gay studies. (Hyde dedicated the book to his wife, perhaps necessary given the subject matter and the climate of the early 1970s.) Wilde is a key figure in this study, with a poem by Lord Alfred Douglas on the title page and an opening reference to the Wilde trials. Subtitled 'An Historical and Contemporary Survey of Homosexuality in Britain', Hyde contends that 'the Wilde Trials and their aftermath represented the high water mark of popular prejudice against homosexuality in Victorian England, and the anti-homosexual feeling was continued into the Edwardian and neo-Georgian period. A more humanitarian climate was slow in coming.'[20] This version of the Wilde trials and their aftermath will be familiar to readers of his other works, with Hyde presenting Wilde in a sympathetic yet shrewd way. His account of the struggle for reform and the activities of the Wolfenden committee carries him to a final chapter called 'Whither Now?' where he does admit that 'the 1967 Act, which legalised homosexual acts between consenting adults in private, had the immediate effect of encouraging a measure of permissiveness, certainly as regards public discussion, the theatre, radio and television . . . On the other hand, the fear that such permissiveness would lead to more offences in public and against young persons has not been supported by the known facts.'[21] In fact, Hyde draws upon research from the Albany Trust to show that decriminalisation had led to only a slight amelioration of institutional homophobia in the UK and concludes: 'Although there is some considerable way to go yet before homosexuals become fully integrated in the community in Britain, my personal belief is that their complete social acceptance here is only a matter of time.'[22]

Following this groundbreaking study of homosexuality in general in 1975, Hyde's *Oscar Wilde*[23] continued the trend of normalising Wilde and making him safe. Hyde had known Vyvyan Holland well, had interviewed Alfred Douglas and other surviving friends and family of Wilde, and, since many of these people were now dead, Hyde was free to draw on these sources. Hyde expounded the theory, now discredited but given great credence in the 1970s, that Wilde had contracted syphilis from a female prostitute before his marriage and had eventually died of it. Unlike de Vere White, Hyde seems to accept Shaw's uncorroborated theory that Speranza suffered from gigantism and that her physical condition tainted her son's sexual state: 'Undoubtedly there was some truth in his fellow Irishman's diagnosis. "I have always maintained that Oscar was a giant in the pathological sense", wrote Shaw, "and that this explains a good deal of his weakness."'[24]

Despite this, Hyde is sensible about not blaming Speranza for dressing Wilde as a girl but stresses that Wilde started out in life and marriage as a true heterosexual and was 'turned' by Robert Ross: 'Havelock Ellis has expressed the opinion that homosexuality was latent in Wilde's constitution from the very beginning, although it did not become active until he was in his early thirties.'[25] To prove this, Hyde recounts Wilde's platonic love affairs and physical encounters with women, and then introduces his growing interest in homoerotic art and poetics, and the tradition of same-sex love between men. As part of this process of turning, Hyde recounts Wilde's first sexual encounter with Robbie Ross and then his love affair with Alfred Douglas, and makes the shrewd point that

> If Wilde had been content to confine his homosexual relations to Robert Ross and even to Lord Alfred Douglas, it is extremely unlikely that his conduct in this respect would ever have come to the notice of the Director of Public Prosecutions. Unfortunately for him, he made the fatal mistake of extending his range of his homosexual acquaintances to such individuals as a groom, an unemployed clerk and a newspaper boy.[26]

Hyde does not repeat the old story about Speranza as the primary cause of Wilde's staying in the Cadogan Hotel to face arrest and is refreshingly sceptical about Bosie's later claims not to have enjoyed sex with men. Hyde finishes his unsensational account of Wilde's life by quoting Shaw:

> Please let us hear no more of the tragedy of Oscar Wilde . . . Oscar was no tragedian. He was the superb comedian of his century, on to whom misfortune, disgrace, imprisonment were external and traumatic. His gaiety of soul was invulnerable: it shines through the blackest pages of *De Profundis* as clearly as his funniest epigrams. Even on his deathbed he found in himself no pity for himself, playing for the laugh with his last breath, and getting it with as sure a stroke as in his palmiest prime.[27]

Drawing on familiar tropes around Wilde the Irish rebel, Ulick O'Connor reviewed Hyde's book in the *Sunday Independent* in an article called 'Why Oscar Chose to Face the Music': 'Irishmen didn't run away from the English and that was that . . . Wilde was crucified, in part, because he could not stand the hypocrisy of the English Establishment. . . . Having made his stand, it is possible that he was unable to resist the Irish appetite for martyrdom.'[28] Interestingly, the novelist John Broderick, writing in the same newspaper about the same book, takes the opposite view. Broderick, born in Athlone in 1924, was a novelist of some note and his novels, including *The Pilgrimage* (1961) and *The Waking of Willie Ryan* (1965),[29] were all groundbreaking works where homosexuality was portrayed as an integral part of a wider spectrum of sexualities for his characters.

For some years now, he has been deified in the literary sense: and since one encounters criticism of his work, as distinct from his personality and trials, it might be salutary to point out that his writing, apart from one play, is second rate and often worse. On the whole he is a very bad writer indeed . . . Wilde had not genius: he was deluding himself if he imagined he had a high social position and he had no intellectual daring whatsoever . . . He was the prototype of those Irish men and women who go to England, determined to make their name at any cost . . . I think it is not too much to say that he deliberately chose jail and exile at the height of his career; but there is small doubt that subconsciously at any rate, he brought ruin on himself . . . Everything gets full and detailed treatment, including aspects of Wilde's sexual life which, not to put too fine a point on it, are disgusting. Does it really add to one's knowledge of anyone to examine bed linen?[30]

Broderick's antipathy to Wilde is surprising given that he would go on to write a rarity in Irish writing, a novel, *The Trial of Father Dillingham* (1989), where two men live as a couple, are clearly sexual partners and are permitted reflection on the nature of their sexual identity and their place within a wider Irish culture. Several factors permitted Broderick the possibility to be open and frank as a writer about homosexuality at this time in Ireland. His first book, *The Pilgrimage*, was banned in 1961, partly because of the theme of homosexuality, but he continued to publish on this theme because he had an independent family income. In interviews, Broderick distanced himself from the homosexual theme:

I think the Irish are pathological about homosexuality. That was one of the reasons why I chose it as the theme for my books because it never had been done before. It existed in a small way in the bourgeoisie in Ireland. I think probably much more now. But it was one of the things which were absolutely unspeakable and which they would never admit to, so if you wanted to hit them that was where to hit them . . . He's [Proust] now discussed quite openly in universities. And Wilde is, but it would not have happened in Wilde's lifetime.[31]

This makes Broderick's antagonism towards Wilde in the *Irish Independent* review all the more surprising, but, perhaps, as he never came out himself, his lack of sympathy for Wilde's exposure and criminality, the idea that he 'brought ruin on himself', may have fuelled his antagonism. I would suggest a parallel in Colm Toibín's novel *The Master*, where Wilde acts as a warning and a reproach.

Broderick's friend, the poet and critic John Jordan,[32] reviewed Rupert Hart-Davis's *The Letters of Oscar Wilde* in the Irish journal *Hibernia* in 1979 and was much more benign about Wilde:

Society, nineteenth-century English society, decided to brand him as
an animal. And even now, sixty years after his death, his name has an
irrelevant aura of sinister notoriety, though we should all know by
now that Oscar Wilde is a classic instance of the scapegoat or the
whipping boy . . . For most of this review I have concentrated on
'Wilde' rather than 'Oscar'. But I am not insensitive to 'Oscar' and
that incorrigible, some might say unforgivable, gaiety of spirit that
sustained him even to the gates of death.[33]

Jordan, a friend also of Kate O'Brien and of mac Líammóir and Edwards,
was part of a younger generation of Irish writers in the 1960s and 1970s
challenging and remaking the boundaries of Irish writing and, as this
happened, cultural perceptions around homosexuality were changing,
particularly in the 1970s as Irish lesbians and gay men became politicised
in line with new ideas around gay consciousness and gay liberation.

From the mid-1970s onwards, the National Gay Federation in Dublin
produced news-sheets and monthly newsletters as part of consciousness-
raising for Irish lesbians and gay men in the campaign for
decriminalisation. In the early 1980s, they published a monthly magazine
called *Identity*, with essays, short stories, film reviews and political features. One significant aspect of this journal's remit was a series of research
articles on Irish gay history,[34] with a feature on the Atherton case in
December 1982 and another on male homosexuality in Gaelic Ireland
in March 1983.[35] Each of these well-researched and lively essays made
the point that gay subcultures had already existed, claiming a genealogy
of Irish queerness to support the emergence of a contemporary gay identity in Ireland. Wilde was claimed as part of this genealogy with an essay
by Richard Pine in the April–June issue in 1983, and the series concluded with essays on the Dublin Castle scandal and on the case of the
unfortunate Bishop of Clogher in September 1983. Wilde was, already, a
symbol of the politicisation of Irish lesbians and gays.
    New Irish studies on Wilde, gradually more and more open-minded,
continued to appear. Richard Pine's short study, *Oscar Wilde*, was published in 1983 and was, in Pine's own words, 'An opportunity to write
about Wilde as an Irishman . . . the dichotomy of the Anglo-Irishman, the
homosexual and the artist in the mid-to-late nineteenth century.[36] Owen
Dudley Edwards's original and lively study, *The Fireworks of Oscar Wilde*,
was published in 1989 and is important for an evolving sense of Wilde as
Irish in that he connects Irishness and sexuality.[37] Dudley Edwards suggests that, in *The Importance of Being Earnest*, '"earnest" was their secret
code-name for what is now generally termed "gay" . . . To the world at
large, it must have seemed the most anti-climactic of all the succession of

fireworks, in themselves the most brilliant and most scientifically deployed of all Wilde's pyrotechnical displays on the theatre stage. But to the homosexual audience, it would be the finest and Wildest firework of all.'[38] He also suggests that 'He is a case study of Irish immigration into Britain for the entire official Union of the two islands.'[39]

A critical conjunction of Irish gay present and homosexual past came in October 1992 when David Norris delivered 'The Green Carnation and the Queer Nation – Oscar Wilde Reclaimed',[40] a commemorative lecture in memory of Oscar Wilde, commissioned by the postgraduate common room of Trinity College Dublin. Norris opens with his own evolving sense of Wilde as an Irish gay precursor.

> I had until recently a disinclination to bother myself very much with Oscar Wilde and his work as he seemed to me the epitome of the dilettantist – as social butterfly, effete and irrelevant, whose catastrophe was precipitated by an incorrigibly foolish attempt to play out the real life drama of his trial as if it were a scene out of one of his own drawing room comedies. Moreover because I was gay, an interest in Wilde and his circle was often automatically assumed.[41]

Norris examines his own initial lack of connection to Wilde (he was much better known as a Joycean) and argues:

> My thesis tonight is that far from being a disadvantage, merely the catalyst of his tragedy, Wilde's unorthodox sexuality was an important and fundamental source of his genius . . . Making him, as I have belatedly come to realize, a fitting and heroic icon for the gay movement.[42] . . . When that moment came and the mask finally slipped away revealing his true identity, at the point of his greatest degradation, he took charge of his destiny by a triumphant assertion of the will and of the imagination. In doing so, he became entitled to rank among the first great figures of gay liberation . . . I do not claim Wilde exclusively for the gay community – to do so would be to blaspheme against his essential humanity.[43]

Norris came to Wilde, not as a literary critic but as a politically active Irish gay man. From Trinity College came a slightly less radical reclaiming of Wilde with Davis Coakley's 1994 study *Oscar Wilde: The Importance of Being Irish*,[44] a balanced and sensible study of Wilde in the year after decriminalisation of male homosexuality in Ireland. In this study, Coakley is anxious to reclaim Wilde's Irishness in every way but one. He introduces the topic of homosexuality only at the end of his narrative and then simply as a foreign vice. (Recent evidence by Neil McKenna suggests that Wilde was sexually active with other men before his marriage, or at least involved with homoerotic culture.)[45] Coakley claims Wilde's creative vitality as Irish, and quotes Wilde's Irish American friend Vincent O'Sullivan, who wrote, 'Oscar Wilde's genius was essentially . . . Irish'.[46] Coakley writes of Sir William and Jane Wilde thus: 'Their eccentricities were highlighted and their faults exaggerated by biographers in an attempt to explain or mitigate their son's behaviour.'[47] Coakley sensibly refuses to participate in any demonising of the Wilde parents; instead he strengthens his argument about the importance of Wilde's Irishness by taking seriously their scholarship in the areas of folklore and antiquities.

The main focus of the Coakley book is to find Irish influences and sources for Wilde's writings. He respects Speranza's importance within Irish literary culture but makes the shrewd point that Wilde did not actually inherit his mother's nationalism in any active sense. 'Wilde once described himself as a "most recalcitrant patriot" in a letter in which he avowed his home rule sympathies . . . he shrank from fanatical patriotism'.[48] Coakley recounts the tale that Wilde's name was taken off the Portora honours board. The story of Wilde's homosexuality comes late in Coakley's book, and as something menacing: 'Beautiful imagery or an appropriate phrase could conceal unsavoury realities; but not indefinitely. As rumours spread, Wilde ignored advice to moderate his behaviour.'[49] He excused his extravagance on the basis that the 'virtues of prudence and thrift were not in my own nature or my own race'.[50] The familiar code of Anglo-Irish pride and folly is evoked around Wilde's downfall, and Parnell, Yeats and Heaney are deployed to connect Wilde with a seamless genealogy of Irishmen at odds with the British establishment. Oakley makes much of Wilde's post-prison attraction towards Catholicism and his deathbed conversion, and ends with Lennox Robinson's speech at the unveiling of the Wilde birthplace plaque, a safe and unchallenging way in which to reclaim Wilde's rashness.

In the 1990s, scholars of Irish writing rediscovering Wilde the Irishman in the aftermath of decriminalisation did so in the face of an earlier tendency to write Wilde out of the canon of Irish literature. In his influential study *The Irish Comic Tradition*, published in 1962, Vivian Mercier signalled that 'I have virtually ignored many of the Anglo-Irish writers who neither lived most of their lives in Ireland nor continued to write much about Ireland after they had left her . . . Shaw, Wilde, Sheridan . . . belong essentially to English literature'.[51] Seamus Deane is more inclusive in his 1986 *A Short History of Irish Literature*, validating Wilde via Yeats: 'The relentlessness of Shaw's and Wilde's attacks on the English middle-classes provided Yeats with the opportunity to convert their cosmopolitanism into his own peculiar brand of literary nationalism. Wilde's languid dandyism was converted by Yeats into images of historical catastrophe.'[52] Deane takes Wilde seriously as a political exemplar for Yeats, yet he does so without any direct discussion of homosexuality.

Gradually, in the 1990s, Wilde was welcomed back into the fold of approved Irish writing. In 1994, the proceedings of a conference held the previous year at the Princess Grace Library in Monaco called 'Rediscovering Oscar' were published under the editorship of C. George Sandulescu, drawing on a wide range of Irish and international scholars. Neil Sammells's essay 'Rediscovering the Wilde Irish' provides a fascinating context for contemporary Irish critical views on Wilde.

> G.J. Renier notes in his 1933 half-crown biography that Wilde 'was not effeminate. He was powerful, robust, and Irish' . . . However his insistence on Wilde's Irishness was double-edged. He can employ it to rescue Wilde from one accusation but only by levelling another. Renier says of Wilde's sexual preferences that the homosexual temperament was present in him to a fairly marked degree, though not to such an extent as it prevented marriage and procreation: 'but' – and here, so to speak, is the rub – 'upon this temperament was superimposed a lack of self-control due to his nationality'.[53]

Sammells reads Irish versions of Wilde, analysing the overlap between nation and sexual identity.

> This series of sliding identifications is crucial to Wilde and to our understanding of the importance to him of both his nationality and his nationalism . . . His penchant for the green carnation is symptomatic. It is the badge of a homosexual coterie, a demonstration of the self-consciously modern and refined taste which prefers the artificial to the natural, and a declaration of national allegiance which refracts and politicises both.[54]

Sammells demonstrates the ways in which the influential *The Field Day Anthology of Irish Writing*[55] in 1991 constructs Wilde as not quite Irish, and as compromised by his 'Englishness', or his contact with English society. (He does exempt Declan Kiberd from this, suggesting that Kiberd is one of the few *Field Day* editors to see the potentially subversive elements within Wilde's writings on England.) Otherwise, in Sammells's own words, 'The compilers of the new canon shift uneasily in their attempts to account for the nature of Wilde's Irishness and for the effect it has upon his work.'[56] Sammells concludes,

> Rediscovering the Irish Wilde is not a matter of excavation, of scraping away the accretions of Englishness to reveal a Celtic core. It is, rather, a matter of recognizing alternative identities simultaneously maintained. Wilde's Irishness is not defeated by his Englishness

– however uncomfortable this might make the Anthologists. Instead the Irish Wilde is defined both by and against the English Wilde.[57]

Perhaps the most influential critic of his generation within Irish studies, Declan Kiberd sees an Irish Wilde, playful, subversive and paradoxical within colonial discourse, and this does much to reclaim him as a figure of postmodern self-invention for contemporary Ireland. In his characteristically accessible, lively and perceptive style, Kiberd creates this version of Wilde in much of his writings in the 1990s, thus locating a new variant on the old Wilde, the Irish rebel at bay in an English court – Wilde the Irish subversive, inverting the empirical certainties of the British establishment. In his selection for *The Field Day Anthology of Irish Writing* Volume 2, in 1991, Kiberd grouped Wilde with Shaw in his 'London Exiles' section, putting them back into the canon of Irish writing by calling them 'cultural godfathers of the Irish Renaissance'.[58] In his selection of writings here, Kiberd's Wilde is subversive and anti-imperial but not at all sexual, reflecting this idea of Wilde's revolt against the British Empire with texts like *The Happy Prince* and *The Decay of Lying*, the review of Froude and the Dorian Gray paradoxes. Kiberd's Wilde is an attractive, witty inverter of late-Victorian humbug but one firmly desexualised, with no quotes from *Salome* or *De Profundis* or the homoerotic elements of *The Picture of Dorian Gray*. Kiberd expands this sense of Wilde in his 1995 study *Inventing Ireland* with a full chapter, 'Oscar Wilde – The Artist as Irishman', and later in his *Irish Classics* (2000).

Kiberd's version is original in placing Wilde within contemporary postcolonial theory and yet at the same time there is something strangely reductionist, particularly in his account of Speranza's influence on her second son. 'From the outset, her attitude to Oscar was ambivalent. She had longed for a girl and so, when the boy-child arrived like an uninvited guest, she was somewhat miffed. Thereafter, this ardent feminist and radical alternately pampered and neglected him.'[59] (Do we know this? Her letters from this period of her life, Oscar's early childhood, would tend to contradict it.) Kiberd's real contribution to Irish Wildean re-appropriation is in the concept of 'the art of elegant inversion', the idea that Wilde undermined the imperialist relationship between England and Ireland by inverting the assumptions that justified English rule in Ireland:

> The ease with which Wilde effected the transition from stage Ireland to stage England was his ultimate comment on the shallowness of such categories . . . To his mortification and intermittent delight, Wilde found that his English mask was not, by any means a perfect fit. The more he suppressed his inherited personality, the more it seemed to assert itself.[60]

Kiberd is inclined to relegate Wilde's homosexuality to the margins, seeing it as an expression of a kind of intellectual dissent rather than a central physical and sexual identity: 'It is possible to see this cult of inversion as Wilde's private little joke about his own homosexuality but it is much more than that: at the root of these devices is his profound scorn for the extreme Victorian division between male and female, which he saw as an unhealthy attempt to foster an excessive sense of difference between the sexes.'[61] Kiberd's real strength is in his remaking of Wilde within a tradition of Irish subversion of British imperialism:

> The Irish, by way of resistance, could go in either of two ways; and Wilde, being Wilde, went in both. On one side, he duplicated many of the attributes of the colonizer, becoming a sort of urbane, epigrammatic Englishman . . . On another more subversive level, he pointed to a subterranean, radical tradition of English culture, which might form a useful alliance with Irish nationalism and thus remain true to its own deepest imperatives.[62]

Kiberd expands his version of anti-imperialist Wilde in his 2000 book *Irish Classics*[63] with a chapter called 'Anarchist Attitudes: Oscar Wilde'. In this chapter, Kiberd moves on his construction of Wilde to a point where his writings and his aesthetic are derived almost exclusively from his racial origins, springing from a tradition of Gaelic literature of dissent, 'The drawing room figures of Wilde's drama are really the shaughrauns and rogues of nineteenth-century Irish writing brought indoors and civilized: and the play is the zone where the values of the old Gaelic and modern English aristocracies meet. What is under attack in both literatures is the imaginative narrowness of the new middle class.'[64] Kiberd places Wilde within this tradition of Gaelic dissent and then finds links with Wilde and Padraig Pearse, suggesting that 'it would not be fanciful to suggest that the mentality which lay behind the Easter Rising of 1916 – that he who loses life will save it by a Christ-like combination of goodness and social rebellion – is traceable to this thinking. Pearse was hardly the only rebel who had been moved by the tales of Oscar Wilde, which saw in Jesus a conflation of artist and rebel, the scapegoat and the scapegrace.'[65] Kiberd takes Wilde seriously in terms of his flirtation with Catholicism but does not take quite the same attitude to his sexual otherness:

> Wilde never portrayed himself as a gay martyr, least of all to Bosie. 'I am here', he tells him in a letter from jail 'for having tried to put your father in prison'. . . Wilde did not go to jail for homosexuality (except in the most technical sense). His real crime was, in the words of Mary McCarthy, 'making himself too much at home' in English society.

He was the ultimate social nightmare, a self-invited guest who had to be barred.[66]

Kiberd sees Wilde's Irishness as important only in a political sense and not in a sexual sense: 'Even as he wrote *De Profundis* (which he called *Epistula: In Carcere et Vinculis*), Wilde must have been aware that his text would take its place in the long tradition of Irish prison literature.'[67]

The most sustained study of Wilde in Irish studies came in 1995 when Richard Pine published his *The Thief of Reason: Oscar Wilde and Modern Ireland*, an expansion of his earlier brief life of Wilde and the sole work to date that deals in any detailed way with Wilde's sexual and racial character. Pine's original if sometimes opaque study of Wilde places him within the context of new lesbian and gay literary studies and also suggests that Wilde influences the nature of twentieth-century Irishness in a profound and lasting way: 'He was Irish and therefore provincial; homosexual and therefore culpable; artistic without being an artist and therefore risible.'[68] Pine argues that to be Irish in the nineteenth century was to be quintessentially an outsider, and makes the intriguing point that Wilde's Irishness made his gayness unreadable for the English right up to his trials. 'Wilde was a diacrisis in the book of Ireland and the book of the nineteenth century. The age to which he "stood in symbolic relation" was the age of the outsider.'[69] England thus had to be the stage setting for Wilde's performance of his outsider sexuality, his queerness: 'The ambivalence of Irishness, as it was described by nineteenth-century writers, consisted in its powerlessness to achieve reality – to give force as well as character to the state of Ireland – while ironically it was precisely this incapacity which made it unique and unassailable.'[70] Pine dissents from Richard Ellmann's influential 1988 biography of Wilde, particularly from what he sees as Ellmann's unfocused sense of Wilde's homosexuality. Instead he characterised Wilde's inclusive yet contradictory capacities as unmistakably Irish, particularly in his ability to encapsulate and embody contradictions to make a new truth, thus inventing a particularly Irish colonial and modernist strategy.

Pine links Wilde to other transgressive Irish figures within the creation of a modern Irish literary identity, Yeats and Joyce amongst others, and makes the point that 'Wilde's pederasty became as offensively Irish as Parnell's adultery . . . and in both cases, Ireland made of the martyr a saint and a pillar of shame'.[71] Here England, and not Ireland, becomes the site of Wilde's queerness: 'At Oxford, Wilde brought the Irish personality into an arena where homosexuality, religion and the aesthetic were earnestly discussed.'[72]

The strength of Pine's study is his precise delineation of Wilde's Irish background, the influence of a nineteenth-century Irish Protestant tradition of dissent, and also his influence on his Irish successors. However, at the centre of his analysis of Wilde's homosexuality, there is a reductive tendency by Pine to see Wilde's homosexuality as a pose, a colonial strategy, rather than as a core identity driven by desire and by increasing sexual self-confidence. Like Kiberd, Pine falls back on a familiar discourse around the 'hollowness' of the homoerotic by suggesting that 'in place of a home truth by which life should be lived, there was an emptiness which he set out these multiple personae to fill'.[73] Pine's most useful contribution to Irish critical perceptions of Wilde come in his concluding chapters, where he argues that 'Wilde's defeat meant that attitudes towards homosexuality hardened . . . the dandy became an ogre'[74] and concludes that 'Wilde was succeeded by Yeats as a mind in action, by Joyce as a mind in emotion'.[75] However difficult to read, at times, Pine's study of Wilde and modern Ireland does have the virtue of suggesting a new range of possible critical perspectives.

The 1998 essay collection *Wilde the Irishman*, edited by Jerusha McCormack, was another important advance in critical reappraisals of Wilde's Irishness, in that it raised questions around his sexuality and, drawing on Kiberd's study, queried the idea of Wilde's performance of national and sexual identity. McCormack's own essay raises perceptive questions around Wilde, firstly around his national identity – 'Was Wilde Irish or British? The trite answer was that he was both'[76] – and then around his homosexuality: 'What does it mean to be gay – or Irish? Is it something one is born with? Or is it a kind of infection, a state one is culturally induced into? What does the gay – or the Irishman – of a century ago have to do with the gay/Irishman of today?'[77] Drawing on Kiberd, McCormack sees Wilde as 'inventing Ireland as he proceeded to invent himself'[78] but seems to see Wilde's Celticism 'as that which moved him outside conventional moral choice and constraint'.[79] McCormack stresses that it marks a radical turning point in terms of cultural perception to see Wilde as Irish and argues that 'in embracing this fate, Wilde redefined what it means to be Irish',[80] thus acknowledging that contemporary Irish engagement with Wilde's fate is continually being renegotiated:

> Through the mediators of the new political climate, those who have restlessly revised our version of Irish history and those who are, through opening commerce with the extremes of both loyalist and nationalist opinion, expanding the debate on who belongs to this island, the adumbrations of Wilde's ghost may be registered.[81]

Kiberd's essay reiterates his reading of Wilde in *Inventing Ireland* by arguing that he invented himself as English, only to have it rebound on him at the trials. In Kiberd's account, Yeats admired Wilde's snobbery as a strategy for survival. Wilde, always an outsider, was forced to undermine the idea of sincerity because he was Irish in England (Kiberd has a slightly reductive habit here of interpreting the formation of sexual identity as driven by intellectual choice rather than hormonal inclination). However, Kiberd acknowledges that Wilde could never write about the Ireland of his childhood.

In her essay 'Wilde and Orality', Deirdre Toomey traces the sources of Wilde's storytelling and his children's tales back to his parents' folk collecting, thus reinforcing the idea of Wilde the Anglo-Irish writer: 'Oscar Wilde can be associated with those Protestant nationalists (Sir William Wilde, Lady Wilde, Douglas Hyde, Lady Gregory, Yeats, Synge) who, by linking themselves to a despised, indigenous, preliterate culture with folktales and folk parables, re-identified with Ireland.'[82] But, it has to be said that Wilde never directly identified with folk art. Rather he drew on the structures and the tropes of these oral narratives to provide a kind of Gothic subtext for his modern urban tales. Nor did he ever identify with the political purpose of folk art, the revival of cultural nationalism. Bernard O'Donoghue, in 'The Journey to Reading Gaol: Sacrifice and Scapegoat in Irish Literature', offers an original and thoughtful analysis on the precise genealogy of Wilde's idea of sacrifice within the traditions of Irish cultural writing around this potent symbol of martyrdom. Significantly, he links Wilde's idea of sacrifice with that of Padraig Pearse: 'Like Wilde, it was almost totally founded in Christian imagery and terminology.'[83] O'Donoghue argues against the cliché of Irish sacrifice being somehow elemental or pagan, and instead suggests that 'Wilde again offers an enlightening instance of the more specialised way in which the sacrificial victim occurs in Irish writing'[84]. Derek Mahon rereads Wilde as: 'Not some sort of highbrow Noel Coward but in reality a subversive, indeed a revolutionary figure',[85] and goes on, 'The key appears to have been his mother'.[86] 'Lady Wilde had long ago disparaged shame while approving of sin which may have been some consolation.'[87] As the twentieth century closes, Speranza's reputation gains more and more respect and validation in Irish literary culture.

Side by side with these critical and scholarly changes and engagements, the Ireland of the 1990s was reincorporating Wilde into the pantheon of the acceptable. Many other visible signs of Wilde being reclaimed include the Wilde autumn school in Bray, organised by the Wildean scholar David Rose, editor of the online journal *Oscholars*. The Wilde autumn school ran from 1994 until 1997, and speakers included Merlin Holland, Declan Kiberd and Frank McGuinness.

In 1997 the Oscar Wilde statue, commissioned by Guinness Ireland and created in coloured marble by English artist Danny Osborne, then living in Cork, was unveiled in Merrion Square in October 1997. This was the first statue of Wilde in Dublin and, in an article in *The Irish Times* called 'Oscar Comes Out at Last – Within Sight of Home',[88] Eileen Battersby wrote:

> Celebration and muted outrage greeted the unveiling of a new sculpture honouring the writer Oscar Wilde yesterday . . . The response was one of unanimous approval . . . Executed in porcelain, bronze and coloured stones, including jade, pink Norwegian thulite and blue pearl granite, a life-size Wilde sits somewhat languidly, complete with Trinity tie, upon a massive piece of Wicklow quartz. Commissioned by Guinness Ireland, the sculpture cost £45,000. While the various colours, texture and extraordinarily realistic detail ensure that it is difficult to keep one's eyes off the work, Osborne's greatest achievement may well be Wilde's facial expression, a mixture of wry amusement and deep, almost stern sadness – depending on which angle one views it from. The powerful statue is flanked by two black granite plinths with bronzes representing art and life, the one depicting Dionysus; the other a figure of a pregnant woman, that of Constance, Oscar's wife, representing life . . . After Wilde's grandson, Mr Merlin Holland, had performed the unveiling of the statue, attention was drawn to one of the individual quotes adorning the pillar of life: 'that little tent of blue which prisoners call the sky'. This was the quotation from Wilde which most captivated one Charles J. Haughey on selecting it more than two years ago. Wilde had to wait almost a century.[89]

The unveiling of the statue led to a letter to *The Irish Times*:

> Sir, The Municipal Gallery of Modern Art is presently exhibiting a fine tribute to Oscar Wilde. What surprises me, however, is that a Dublin gallery should introduce his exhibition by stating that Oscar was born in Dublin and graduated from Oxford. No mention of Trinity College. Furthermore, it states that his native city has no monument to Oscar, so ignoring the fine statue in Merrion Square. I ask what kind of statements are these in Oscar's own birthplace. Finally, why is our Municipal Gallery asking visitors to contribute to the erection of a monument to Oscar in England? Yours, etc., Noel MacCanna.[90]

Noreen Doody recounts other examples of Wilde's new cultural visibility:

> The various public commemorations include a stained glass window of the Happy Prince by artist, Peader Lamb, commissioned by Dublin's Oscar Wilde Society in 1995. . . . In Galway city a monument depicting Oscar Wilde in conversation with Eduard Vilde stands in the centre of the city. This sculpture was presented to the

people of Galway by the people of Tartu, Estonia in celebration of the Day of Welcomes for the new accession states to the EU.[91]

Trinity College Dublin reclaimed Wilde when, in 1998, the Oscar Wilde Centre for Irish Writing was opened. Its website tells us that 'the Centre was originally the home of the Wilde family and it was in the Westland Row house that the famous son of Sir William and Lady Wilde ("Speranza") was born on October 16th 1854. As a fitting tribute to one of Trinity College's best known students, the Oscar Wilde Centre will eventually house a library and reading room dedicated to his memory.'[92] This centre was the venue for a conference called 'The Wilde Legacy' in 2000, the hundredth anniversary of his death.

Other centenary events in Ireland included an RTÉ Radio Thomas Davis lecture series, which took place between January and March 2000, with Merlin Holland, Declan Kiberd and others as speakers. RTÉ Television screened a series of programmes on Wilde in October, RTÉ Radio broadcast a series of readings of his poems and plays, and Wilde poems were posted up on Dublin's DART commuter trains. For Gay Pride, at the end of June 2000 in *The Irish Times*, Medb Ruane in an essay called 'Dáil Should Come out of the Closet for Pride Week' made the point that 'Irish identity is still reluctant to include its gay and lesbian citizens' and called Wilde 'a dead gay hero'.[93] A re-imagining of Wilde was now possible with all of these changes in political and scholarly perceptions of the once shadowy figure.

6. Imagining Wilde
the Irishman:
1980–2000

The options of Irishness at the end of the twentieth century reflect a great dislocation. (R.F. Foster)[1]

The last years of the twentieth century saw a remaking of the ways in which Ireland defined itself as a newly wealthy Europeanised liberal society and, for writers, this led to an expansion of the acceptable areas for mainstream creativity and new imaginative territories reflecting this social and cultural change. Fintan O'Toole writes: 'In the last decade of the century, the Republic embraced another form of globalisation so thoroughly that it came to represent an extreme manifestation of the phenomenon.'[2] In Irish writings, marginal discourses, homosexuality for one, now became much more public and central as the law changed and, as the critic Linden Peach suggests,[3] 'previously marginalized groups, albeit not entirely free of their marginalized social, physical and cultural status, bring about a revisioning of the nation's map in terms of margins and centres'.[4]

This revisioning of the nation's map meant that key figures of difficulty like Wilde were now re-appropriated as new symbols of unreflective modernity and post-imperialism within Irish writing. The critic Gerry Smyth queries this unquestioned revisioning for contemporary Irish fictive voices and he does so in the light of a colonised past. He asks: 'How can the colonized subject articulate differences without metamorphosing into the image of that which she/he opposed?'[5] Smyth argues that, 'As critical strategies, the liberal and radical modes guarantee that the subaltern cannot speak, for speaking in those modes always entails an acknowledgement, however remote or tacit, of the agenda preset by the colonizing power'.[6] Wilde, once implicated with anti-colonial strategies and then sidelined in the new Ireland, was now seen as a token of postmodernity. Noreen Doody writes that:

> . . . Wilde, who once lamented that not being talked about was a far worse thing than being talked about would have no reason to complain on this account in relation to his current reception in Ireland: he is regularly quoted, his plays are continually in performance on the amateur and professional stage and he is endlessly discussed in the print and digital media.[7]

However, this new visibility has its many nuances, depending on the use to which Wilde's name is being deployed. In these last two chapters, I want to query this idea of a contemporary awareness of Wilde and suggest instead that, in the creative sphere, the familiar misconceptions around his homosexuality lurk underneath the surface of this new version of Wilde, our contemporary, the man of wit and subversion for the twenty-first century speaking to our own remade selves.

As seen in the last chapter, Irish institutions that had silenced Wilde's name, like Trinity College or Portora Royal College, in the 1990s used him as an emblem of liberalisation and inclusiveness, and his name now stood as a kind of shorthand for tolerance and acceptance. This is not unique to Irish culture. As Glyn Davis writes, in relation to contemporary British queer cinema:

> Over the last decade, a variety of writers (many of whom could be cat-egorised as queer theorists) have argued, retroactively, for Oscar Wilde's radicalism. Indeed many of them have claimed that Wilde should be interpreted as proto-queer . . . His radical status must surely be undermined or partially offset, for instance, by his class associa-tions and by the canonisation of his work as literature.[8]

Wilde was refashioned in the light of contemporary cultural needs, despite any real sense of Wilde's own class associations or his sense of himself as an outcast. This is also true for Wilde's supposed Irish Republicanism, where his intentions and credentials were irrelevant to his subsequent cul-tural position, so that Wilde the Irish gay rebel was now being constructed in light of contemporary imaginative pressures and needs. Declan Kiberd suggest that 'the Irish know, better than most peoples, that the attempt by a post-colony to modernise is a painful and uneven process'.[9] In this chapter, I consider the fictive and dramatic representations of Wilde's life and his work and the uneven ways in which he is employed as an icon of modernity and inclusiveness in the dramas of Terry Eagleton and Thomas Kilroy and in the screenplay of Barry Devlin.

To gain a context on the changing perceptions of Wildean sexual dif-ference, it is worth considering 'Dramas', a short story published by the novelist Edna O'Brien in 1989 in the *Paris Review*. The story reflects this sense of a recovered 'queer' Irish past and deploys Wilde directly as a transgressive icon in this story of homosexuality and its containment in rural Ireland. Set in a small Irish town in the 1950s and drawing from O'Brien's own upbringing in rural County Clare, the story is told by the narrator, a teenage girl, who is befriended by Barry, a local shopkeeper. Barry is much liked by the narrator and the older women of the town, giving away free biscuits and unlimited credit in his clean, modern shop and available for hours of gossip and fun. Barry is clearly encoded as gay, making no sexual demands on the young girl and providing a listening ear for all her troubles. His sexuality is also hinted at by his interest in Chekhov and Strindberg, also shared by the young girl, and the link between the two is that of aesthetic longing and preoccupation. The denouement of the story comes when Barry writes to a famous Irish actor in Dublin about a play that he wants to perform. This actor is clearly based on Micheál mac Líammóir for, when talking about the letter, Barry declaims to his mystified customers, 'All for Hecuba and Hecuba for me',[10] an intertextual reference to the title of mac Líammóir's memoir. The unnamed Dublin actor turns up in the small town with his 'friend' Ivan (Hilton, perhaps). Then all three men proceed to get drunk in Barry's house and put on dresses and wigs, to the delight and mock-horror of an assembled mob of locals outside the house, attracted by the noise. The name of Wilde is invoked during this transgressive cross-dressing saturnalia: 'then he said something awful: he said that the great Oscar Wilde had termed marriage "the sheets of lawful lust".'[11] The local policeman is called in and tries to gain entry to the house, to the delight and delectation of the three drunken men. They end up kissing him, and then a group of local men intervene and eject the three men from the town. As he is being led away, Barry looks imploringly at his former protégée, the female narrator, and the story ends with her rejection of her former friend. For the village girl, Barry's closeted sexuality is now too openly displayed to be tolerated and the mood of the story turns from comedy to regret by the narrator at her betrayal of her former friend, now a Wildean outcast. However, despite the routing and expelling of the three gay men, they inhabit a world of art and drama that is envied by the young female narrator, and also feared. O'Brien tilts the story in favour of the gay men by suggesting that this is an escape from the rural closet into a queer metropolitan subculture, a refuge from the constraints of heterosexuality into a sub-Wildean world. Much of the sympathy of the story is directed towards the hapless Barry and the excitingly shameless visitors from the Dublin metropolis.

Another contemporary Irish writer, Seamus Heaney, as already quoted, sees Wilde as an example of resistance and courage in the light of his Irishness and he celebrates Wilde's place within the tradition of the Irishman at bay in the English courtroom, facing down British justice with style. In his 1995 essay 'Speranza in Reading Gaol', he writes that 'during his trials in 1895, Wilde had been magnificent in the dock and conducted himself with as much dramatic style as any Irish patriot ever did'.[12] Heaney, introducing *The Ballad of Reading Gaol* on RTÉ Radio in 1992, also suggested that:

At this distance in that particular light, there is indeed a way of seeing
Oscar Wilde as another felon of our land, another prisoner in an
English jail so that the ballad then becomes the link in a chain
including John Mitchel's *Jail Journal* and Brendan Behan's *The Quare
Fella*, prison literature. This poem written by the son of Speranza . . .
may be devoid of Irish nationalist political intent but it is full of subversive anti-Establishment sentiment. It has about it a kind of high
banshee lament, the voice of one crying in the wilderness.[13]

In his dedication speech in Westminster Abbey on 14 February 1995
Heaney takes up this theme again, seeing Wilde in the tradition of resistance writing and anti-imperialism:

The cry of hurt is every bit as audible in the *Ballad of Reading Gaol*
as it is in the song of St James's Infirmary although the provenance of
Wilde's chain-gang poem is Irish rather than American and looks
back to all the convict ballads, gaol journals and political poetry of
Irish nationalist literature in the nineteenth century – a literature in
which Wilde's mother famously contributed under the pseudonym
of Speranza. But if it looks back to Irish patriots in the dock for felony
in Dublin and an Irish playwright in the dock for homosexuality in
London, it also looked forward to English soldier-poets in the
trenches in Flanders.[14]

Seamus Heaney was also linked with the artistic project Field Day, a
Derry-based artistic co-operative of actors, writers, critics and musicians pro-
ducing plays, pamphlets and studies around questions of Irish cultural
nationalism from the 1980s onwards. The critic and writer Terry Eagleton's
play *Saint Oscar* was a Field Day project and a revealing version of Wilde
from within the tradition of Irish cultural nationalism. Peter Dickinson has
written that 'Oscar Wilde has, of course, repeatedly been subjected to
posthumous conscription by scholars, critics, writers, and artists as the
exemplary literary, sexual, and national outlaw',[15] and here I want to
examine the way in which Eagleton's conscription of Wilde's life finds itself
caught between the contradictions between Wilde's potential as
Republican icon and the unruly nature of Wilde's sexual otherness.

In the 1989 *Saint Oscar*, a play produced by Field Day for the Irish
stage, Eagleton brings Wilde back to 'life', making him the central character in a lively and inventive comic presentation. In the play, the link
between Wilde's dissident sexuality and his potential for a kind of colonial subversion is established and explored as the drama unfolds and, in
the words of Lucia Kramer, 'Eagleton's drama *Saint Oscar* (1989) dispenses with historical details almost altogether and concentrates instead
on theoretical issues'.[16] The English-born Eagleton writes Wilde from a
position of identification with Ireland and his play was produced within

the context of a contemporary and stormy moment in Anglo-Irish relations. In an article in *The Irish Times* about the play, it is explained that 'While he [Eagleton] didn't set out to write an allegory of the present-day Anglo-Irish situation, he found it impossible to write about past conflicts between England and Ireland without reflecting them, if only indirectly, to what is happening today . . . Words he put in Oscar's mouth have a pert and ironic ring in the post-Guildford haze [the Guildford Four].'[17] Eagleton himself writes in his introduction that 'Wilde's treatment at the hands of a brutal, arrogant British establishment is being acted out once more in Ireland today.[18]

With this political foregrounding, Eagleton thus dispenses with linear progression, in his construction of Wilde's life and his writings. Here, Wilde arbitrarily discourses with those central to his life – Speranza, Bosie and Edward Carson. *Saint Oscar* represents Wilde's homosexuality in a much more direct and subversive way than any previous play, reflecting societal changes in Ireland in the late 1980s, and Eagleton's version of Wilde is promising in terms of the anticipated fusion of sexuality and radical political potential. In the introduction he mentions 'Two factors that had triggered my fascination with Wilde – his Irishness and his remarkable anticipation of some present-day theory'[19] and goes on to mention Foucault. However Eagleton's other comments in his introduction signal his authorial distancing from Wilde's sexuality:

> Much previous work on Wilde has centred on his homosexuality . . . but if I have tried to avoid writing a gay play about him, this is not only because as a heterosexual I am inevitably something of an outsider in such matters but because it seems to me vital to put that particular ambiguity or doubleness back in the context of a much wider span of ambivalence.[20]

This ambivalence towards Wilde's sexuality permeates the play and reflects the ways in which Rebel Wilde had always subsumed the spectre of Queer Wilde in previous works and still does so here. This lively and engaging drama is direct and even celebratory of Wilde's subversive status as a colonial jester in London – 'a parodist and parasite'[21] – and Wilde's undermining of British cultural imperialism is the main focus. The bawdy, often witty, sexually explicit tenor of the play is demonstrated by the opening ballad: 'The moral of our tale is plain for to tell: / Unnatural practices land you in hell / If you're Quare and you're Irish and wear a daft hat. / Don't go screwing the son of an aristocrat.'[22]

Much of the play celebrates Wilde as playful political subversive in his discussions with Richard Wallace and his arguments with Edward Carson. Indeed, in his encounters with Carson, Eagleton anticipates the founding of the state of Northern Ireland and the creation of a bleak, even nightmarish world of biblical intransigence and oppression when Wilde seeks and fails to counter Carson's dark vision of the future Ulster. As Peter Dickinson writes, 'In Eagleton's construction of him, Oscar thus joins a long list of Irish writers, orators, and politicians brought down by a British cultural oligarchy that saw the seductiveness of their language and message as threatening and subversive.'[23] However, this construction of Wilde as sexual rebel, victim of British justice and champion of an enlightened Irish future clashes with his representation of the cause of Wilde's homosexuality and it is significant that all dramatic discussion and debate around the 'cause' and origin of his sexual nature are confined to Wilde's first encounter, that with his mother, a hostile, figure in this version.

The opening scene is in line with many earlier, more hostile versions of Wilde's life, where the over-mothering of Speranza is held accountable for the 'unnatural' homosexuality of her son. In an effort to come to terms with Wilde's sexuality, Eagleton relies on an androgynous notion of sexuality and, in doing so, he falls back on a retrograde feminising of the homoerotic and a discourse of the monstrous to represent sexual otherness. Right at the opening of the play, Wilde describes his first moments of life as 'a monstrous birth. When they pulled me out they screamed and tried to kill me on the spot. A cock and a cunt together, the one tucked neatly within the other.'[24] In the play, it is the mother, Speranza, who is blamed for this hermaphroditic birth, as Wilde accuses her, 'who was it unmanned me?' He goes on to explain: 'Don't you see, mother, something went awry with me within the furry walls of your womb. Your little boy is flawed, botched, unfinished. I had my own body but I was too greedy for flesh. I wanted yours, too. The two don't mix well.'[25] The play thus falls back on the conservative notion that to be homosexual, other, subaltern, all gay men must somehow want to be female, conflating notions of transgendering with the homoerotic to the detriment of both. To be queer might be politically subversive in this play, but it is also seen as sexually monstrous.

In the play, there is a problematic disjunction between the celebration of Wilde's political potential for radicalism and the representation of his unnatural sexuality, the subversiveness of one being undermined by the regressive gendering of the other. Connected with this is Eagleton's unequivocal portrayal of Bosie as a pernicious influence on Wilde – 'I love him . . . as Saint Sebastian loved the arrows'[26] – but is even-handed in demonstrating Wilde's own deliberate courting of his trials and his fall from grace.

As Eagleton constructs Wilde, disgrace was the only place for him to go, the only logical end to his stance of transgression and subversion. Eagleton finds a kind of gallows humour in all this and celebrates Wilde's sabotaging of British imperialism, but, despite all of this, he still draws on traditional and limiting notions of sexual difference. As in all texts about Wilde written in the tradition of Irish nationalist history, Oscar the rebel predominates, but it is to Eagleton's credit that in 1989, when homosexuality was still criminalised in Ireland, he attempts to celebrate the subversive queerness of Wilde. The disjunction between his representation of his sexuality and of his politics is, in fact, an inevitable consequence of the tradition in which he is writing, a nationalist discourse when the erotic is always subaltern, always suspect. In the review in *The Irish Times*, David Nowlan says: 'Mr Eagleton has tried to personify Wilde the person outcast from family, nation and sex, the nation-victim of another establishment. But the parable does not work dramatically.'[27] It does not work because there is no place for a progressive queer Wilde within an Irish nationalist tradition, or at least not at this point. Jamie O'Neill in his novel *At Swim, Two Boys* addresses this very imaginative problem with greater success.

Theatre practice in Ireland continued as a potent force in the remaking of Wilde at the end of the twentieth century. For example, the playwright Frank McGuinness acknowledges Wilde as an influence despite, as he suggests: 'I don't know if you can see Wilde as influencing you as a playwright because the perfection of *The Importance of Being Earnest* is so self-contained and so rightly narcissistic that I don't think you can do anything other than stand back and gaze in amazement.'[28] McGuinness, in an essay called 'The Spirit of Play in Oscar Wilde's *De Profundis*', also suggests that Wilde sees Christ as an Irishman and continues the notion of the Wildean parallel for Irish theatre.[29] In terms of the continuing theatrical engagement with Wilde, the writer Thomas Kilroy produced a drama on the life of Oscar Wilde in the late 1990s that involved a radical reinterpretation of the Wilde family saga and a re-addressing of the relationship between the sexual and the domestic that marked a real sea change in the idea of the Irish family. Drawing on debates within Irish society about domestic worlds, the changing role of women within Irish cultural life and the gradual revelations around hidden sexual lives, he rewrote the Wilde story to focus, for the first time, on Constance Wilde. He interrogates Wilde's homosexuality from the perspective of the family and within the context of the heterosexual marriage.

As a playwright, Kilroy himself had already addressed the theme of homosexuality in his play *The Death and Resurrection of Mr Roche*, a controversial work rejected by the Abbey Theatre but staged with great success during the 1968 Dublin Theatre Festival. It enjoyed further success in London, on radio and television and in translation and was groundbreaking for the Irish stage in its portrayal of a homophobic attack on the gay protagonist, Mr Roche, by a group of his friends, themselves ill-at-ease and unhappy in their own fragile sense of their heterosexuality. The play turns the homophobia and paranoia right back at this group of men and ends up with the apparent resurrection of the formerly 'dead' Mr Roche, back to life, at ease with himself and undamaged. Kilroy's ability to create drama to unsettle the heterosexual norms of the Irish stage can be seen clearly in his version of the Wilde story.

In an interview in *The Irish Times* in October 1997 called 'Kilroy Is Here', he explains his ideas:

> In *The Secret Fall of Constance Wilde*, Constance Holland Lloyd, betrayed wife and disillusioned romantic, asserts herself and confronts her husband, forcing him to acknowledge the squalor behind the epigrams. 'You never face the situation as it really is,' she says, 'Never! Nothing exists for you unless it can be turned into a phrase' ... For Kilroy this is not, despite its historical context, a historical play. It is more concerned with two individuals and their contrasting views of the truth as well as 'trying to present two very different views of normality.[30]

The Secret Fall of Constance Wilde is, dramatically, an intense and often traumatic representation of Wilde's life from the perspective of his wife Constance. In the play, Wilde's fall into sexual sin and the inevitability of his public disgrace is connected to a secret darkness that haunts Constance. Kilroy brings into the familiar historical narrative of Wilde's life a new element, sexual abuse. In Kilroy's version, Constance Lloyd is drawn towards Wilde and marries him, perhaps as a consequence of sexual abuse in childhood. Usually seen as the victimised good wife, here Constance is represented as a strong-willed, clear-sighted woman, resisting the label of good wife or victim and, as the play unfolds, the ugly reality of Wilde's other life, his homosexual affair, becomes entangled with Constance's dark secret and the tainted legacy of her past, her secret fall:

> You – I. All connected. Everything connected. You know I was unable to face that – thing without you being by my side? I used to think: nothing can touch me, married to this brilliant, outrageous man! I am safe beneath this glittering surface! Whereas the truth was you were drawing me into horror, step by step, like a dangerous guide, the horror of myself.[31]

It seems to me that the strength of the Kilroy play is in the rebalancing of the gender roles within the Wilde/Constance/Bosie ménage à trios, but, as with Eagleton's play, Wilde's homosexuality is interpreted as an impulse towards androgyny, a supposed yearning for the fusion of male and female together. Kilroy has Wilde declaim: 'I must have it! I will have it! Neither man nor woman but both . . . The great wound in Nature, the wound of gender, was healed . . . Woman, this is our secret history, the history of the Androgyne.'[32] In Wilde's own writings, this interest in the Androgyne is not particularly evident, Wilde's particular imaginative preoccupations being with absolute beauty and, latterly, with the Christ figure as aesthetic forefather. In Kilroy's version of the central relationships, Bosie is hateful, Wilde is weak, Constance is strong and angry, no longer the passive victimised wife but a woman who has informed herself as to Wilde's real sexual nature and so is not afraid to name it. She tells Bosie: 'You and Oscar are Urnings. That is the term used by the German expert on sexual behaviour, Karl Heinrich Ulrich.'[33] In addition, the bond between Wilde and Constance is seen as a true one and the play ends with the dying Constance writing to her sons, telling them 'But your father is a great man. He had this terrible, strange vision. He sacrificed everything to reach out to that vision.'[34]

The Irish Times review by David Nowlan, titled 'Lives Drily Explored on Sterile Stage', was not enthusiastic:

> Academically, it is near impeccable, this portrayal by Thomas Kilroy of Oscar and Constance Wilde, each prisoners of their own separate conventions, each convention redolent with echoes of the language which either would use, she privately and he publicly. . . . We are listening to a lecture or admiring a demonstration: we are never invited, as a live audience, to engage emotionally in what is going on. The evening is thus, despite the admirable excellence of its component parts, dramatically sterile.[35]

Letters to *The Irish Times* followed this harsh assessment, both agreeing and disagreeing. Titled 'Wilde Play at the Abbey', one visitor from Canada wrote:

> Sir, As a first-time visitor to your amazing city, I feel I must comment on an experience that is for me without parallel. Last Thursday night I was privileged to attend the opening of one of the most remarkable theatrical events in recent memory. *The Secret Life of Constance Wilde* was a treat for both eye and ear. I cannot remember having been so moved as I was by the three very talented actors involved, so touched by a new play, or so stunned by visual beauty. I might add that in my native New York city and my present home in Toronto, I've been an ardent theatre-goer. Upon opening *The Irish Times* next morning, my jaw dropped. If David Nowlan's comments are any reflection of the sophistication and enlightenment of your newspaper, Dublin is in a lot of trouble.[36]

In response, a Dublin theatregoer wrote to support David Nowlan:

> Sir, Having attended with my husband the production of *The Secret Fall of Constance Wilde* at the Abbey Theatre, I would agree with your critic David Nowlan (October 9th) that this production was 'dramatically sterile'. I would go a step further and say that it also was weird, and the whole performance somewhat of a bore. We were going to leave at the interval, but unfortunately decided to stick it out. In the second act there is a scene which depicts Oscar Wilde in prison, kneeling to receive Holy Communion, with Bosie taking the part of the priest. After the Host is administered the priest (Bosie) kisses Oscar on the hands and then on the lips. The significance of this in the context of the production was beyond us and we found it deeply offensive and profane. We have come to rather a new low in theatre in this country. If this is the best our national theatre can give us for our festival, I fear for the future. Yours, etc.[37]

Each of these plays is a hallmark in an evolving perception of Wilde and, by extension, of sexual otherness. Eagleton and Kilroy are more direct in their presentation of his sexuality and they both reinstate dissident sexuality and sexual sin as a central part of the drama of Wilde's life. Only Eagleton allows that sexual sin to be seen as something subversive and radical, whereas Kilroy situates his version of Wilde within a new discourse of trauma, hidden sexual secrets and self-disgust. Neither Kilroy nor Eagleton can quite escape traditional notions of maternal over-nurture and of transgender longings to explain away Wilde's homosexuality, although Kilroy's play does reflect a re-envisioning of the Wilde story with a unique representation of Constance as equal and empowered.

At this time, Wilde also features as a symbol of sexual disturbance in the 1994 film *A Man of no Importance*, written by Barry Devlin and set in Dublin in 1963, at a time when mac Líammóir was playing in *The Importance of Being Oscar*. The central character is called Alfie Byrne and the reference is Joycean for reasons never made clear, Alfie Byrne being a famous Lord Mayor of Dublin. Alfie, a bus conductor, is a middle-aged (closeted and celibate) gay man who lives with his sister and directs productions of Wilde's plays in the local parish hall using his regular customers on the bus. Alfie is encoded as gay with his love of reading, his interest in cooking (even venturing to make spaghetti Bolognese for his bewildered sister) and a strong lisp added to his flat Dublin working-class accent. As the film opens, to the sound of Eartha Kitt singing Cole Porter's 'Let's Fall in Love', Alfie is seen walking alone by the Liffey reading *The Ballad of Reading Gaol* in a strong (exaggerated) Dublin accent and throwing his green carnation into the water. The object of his affections is the handsome young bus driver he works with, Robbie, whom he calls

Bosie, or 'dear boy'. A new production of *Salome* is planned as Alfie's mas-terpiece, and the beautiful young Adele Rice, a country girl newly arrived in Dublin, is immediately claimed as his perfect princess, his Salome.

As the production of *Salome* progresses, the forces of Catholic moral repression in the figures of the local parish priest and the butcher become perturbed about the possibility of 'indecent dancing' and Alfie's produc-tion in the parish hall is threatened with clerical intervention and closure. Wilde's name is constantly evoked within the film, with Alfie quoting Wilde's poems to his early morning passengers, much to the distrust of his Northern Irish supervisor, the crudely drawn villain of the piece. (Indeed most of the characters are crudely drawn, either lovable simpletons quoting Wilde in comic Irish accents or dim-witted moralists without imagination or intelligence seeking to oppose the saintly.) The threat of homosexuality, Alfie's, is the impending revelation of the play, with Wilde as his mentor and warning. At one point, Alfie visits a gay pub in Dublin alone and gazes furtively across the room at a handsome blond man, ter-rified when his gaze is mockingly returned with a theatrical kiss. In another scene, the stupidity of the Irish Catholic moralist is illustrated when discussing the current political scandal of 1963, the Profumo case, where a government minister, John Profumo, was discovered to be sharing a lover with a Russian diplomat. His mistress was introduced to him by a society doctor and homeopath, Stephen Ward, and the right-wing butcher announces to Alfie and his sister that Stephen Ward was guilty of the most serious crime known to humanity, the sin of homeopathy.

In the course of the rehearsals for *Salome*, Alfie begins to come out to his young friend, his Salome, and his sister increases pressure to marry him off and put a stop to the play. The point of crisis comes when he sees his workmate and love object Robbie, his Bosie, in a passionate embrace with a girlfriend. Determined to assert his own sexual identity, Alfie dresses up as Wilde, with a wide-brimmed hat, draped scarf and less than discreet eye make-up, and goes back to the gay bar. 'A queer looking tulip', as one barman remarks, Alfie has made his homosexuality visible by dressing as Wilde (and, perhaps, in imitation of mac Líammóir) and the young gay men in the pub, dressed in contemporary 1960s fashion, react badly. The cruel blond young man, called 'Kitty', responds to Alfie's advances by bringing him outside into the alleyway, where Alfie is beaten and robbed by the gay men. As he lies bleeding, Alfie's gaze lingers on the stars above, a visual pun on one of Wilde's most famous lines, and then he is rescued by a kindly young policeman who laments, 'He's not going to press charges. They never do. The usual thing.'

'As he has learned, by literarily assuming the mantle of gayness in his performance as Wilde, Alfie's desires have become public property',

writes Maria Pramaggiore.[38] Outed by the homophobic attack by other
gay men, Alfie defends his lonely, unrequited passion for the heterosexual
Robbie to his sister: 'The very idea that I might want or love him or ever
feel special towards him would be so repulsive to him that he wouldn't be
able to get far enough away from me . . . Me hands are innocent of affec-
tion.' The cruel bus inspector, now named as Carson, taunts Alfie, telling
him that he should be locked up for what he is. 'I am in prison, I've been
in prison all my life and the one bird that sang to me there through me
prison bars has upped and flown away.' 'Oscar Wilde?' inquires the homophobic Carson. 'Alfred Byrne, I fear', Alfie replies, and, as Carson the bus
inspector retreats, Alfie defends himself by quoting verbatim from Wilde's
speech from the dock defining 'the love that dare not speak its name', to
the applause of his bus passengers.

The film ends as it began, with a reading from *The Ballad of Reading
Gaol*, but, significantly, it is now read by Robbie, Alfie's 'Bosie', who
knows Alfie is gay but tells him 'I don't care what you get up to. I'm your
pal and I know who Bosie was'. The two men rehearse the poem to the
strains of Eartha Kitt singing, 'Let's Fall in Love', Cole Porter's hymn to
the diversity of sexual attraction and desire. Wilde is an enabling figure
for Alfie, a means of coming out, facing down church disapproval and
freeing himself from the strain of his unrequited love for the sympathetic
Robbie. The critic Maria Pramaggiore writes of the film:

> Questions of Ireland's internal diversity are central to the film . . .
> Alfie's fondness for Oscar Wilde situates sexual pluralism at the
> centre of discussions about Irishness in historical and contemporary
> contexts. Because Wilde was Anglo-Irish, and Alfie and his passen-
> gers are Catholic, Alfie's infectious admiration for the playwright
> asserts that Irish artists and national heroes (often one and the same)
> need not be Catholic or heterosexual. Here the reference to the Irish
> theatrical tradition asserts the fact that non-normative subjectivities –
> here, sexual outlaws – have been a part of the modern Irish nation
> and the postmodern Irish Diaspora.[39]

It is true that the availability of Wilde to a Dublin Catholic working-class
man as a symbol of his own sexual identity does indicate a kind of cultural
inclusiveness, but the film projects a retrospective liberalism around
Alfie's gayness, with most of the main (heterosexual) characters sympathetic and tolerant. All clerical homophobia is comical and easily
deflated, and the only real menace and violence comes, ironically, from
other gay men when Alfie impersonates Wilde. (Mac Líammóir's popularity both with a wider Dublin public and within his contemporary gay
community in the 1960s while dressed in a similar manner would undermine such a projection.)

Reviews of the film were not very positive. The *Irish Independent* called it a 'seriously inept movie'.[40] *The Irish Times* carried a review called 'Wild about Oscar', where Michael O'Dwyer wrote: 'But this was a time when "the love that dare not speak its name" was still considered unspeakable, and while the movie displays an affectionate and jovially nostalgic feel for the period, it eschews any predictable "Rare old times" trappings and firmly sets about exposing the bigotry and hypocrisy that lurked beneath the superficial bonhomie.'[41]

Parallel to these texts and new versions of Wilde, new trends in Irish fiction from 1993 meant that a number of Irish writers made their own sexual identity an implicit element within their public persona and, by extension, their own creative voice. For example, when Emma Donoghue, already a literary critic and a cultural historian, published her first novel, *Stir-fry*, in 1994, she did so as an openly lesbian Irish writer. Her literary 'coming out' coincided with the emergence of other openly lesbian and gay Irish writers like Mary Dorcey, Keith Ridgeway and Colm Tóibín, to name a few. When homosexuality was decriminalised in Ireland in 1993, the importance of self-identification for writers in the years after the decriminalisation cannot be under-estimated. Apart from Mary Dorcey, Emma Donoghue was the first openly Irish lesbian writer and this was a radical departure within twentieth-century Irish writing. The most important figure in Irish lesbian writing in the twentieth century up to this point had been her fellow UCD graduate Kate O'Brien, but O'Brien was never visible in terms of her own sexuality, only in terms of her writings. Thus, when Donoghue produced *Stir-fry*, a contemporary Irish coming-out narrative published by Hamish Hamilton, a British imprint, Donoghue was extending the limits of late twentieth-century Irish writing. Before this, lesbian identity within Irish writing had been, to say the least, liminal. Kathryn Conrad contends that within Irish writing to that point:

> The feminist and queer/positive response to occluding or silencing narratives, however, has too often been similarly contained through an implicit acceptance of 'appropriate' or 'significant' topics sanctioned by the patriarchal state; in the public sphere, 'war' and 'government' or in the private sphere, heterosexual romance and personal enlightenment. Resistance means finding new ways to approach narrative, rather than repeating the narrowly focused, carefully contained narrative that ultimately reproduces hierarchies of 'importance'[42]

Donoghue's writings from 1994 onwards suggested a whole range of narrative perspectives and this directly influences the ways in which Wilde is represented. As she put it herself:

> Foreign savours stimulated my appetite, but I hungered for the local.
> The wonderful surveys of lesbian literature I tracked down . . . had
> next to nothing to say about Ireland: they told me about the novels of
> Mary Renault, but not about Kate O'Brien. '*Irish lesbian*' still had the
> ring of a contradiction in terms: how was I to conceive of myself as a
> practising Catholic and a furious lesbian feminist, a sweet colleen
> and a salty sinner?[43]

Thus, in Donoghue's first novel, *Stir-fry* (1994), a witty and likeable college novel set in Dublin, the protagonist, Maria, is a 17-year-old first-year student, an innocent country girl new to city life and to the potential complexities of sexual identity. Her next novel, *Hood*, is a fuller and more sustained examination of an Irish lesbian selfhood and stands, with Kate O'Brien's 1958 novel *As Music and Splendour*, as the most important document of Irish lesbian identity in modern Irish writing. This novel is set in 1992, but, as with *Stir-fry*, the Dublin that it presents is again pre-Celtic tiger, slightly run-down, distinctly non-prosperous. Within this second novel, Donoghue's polarised versions of lesbian identity, hinted at in *Stir-fry*, are much more clearly delineated. These novels signalled new directions within Irish literary culture.

The other important figure in this process of making Irish gay writers visible, commercial and out was Colm Tóibín. In 1993, as he recounts himself, the editor of the *London Review of Books* asked Tóibín to produce a pamphlet 'about my own homosexuality. I told him instantly I couldn't do that. It was a matter, I said, which I did not think I could write about . . . my sexuality was something about which part of me remained uneasy, timid and melancholy.'[44] A gradual coming-out in his fiction and in his literary essays and reviews led to the writing of his influential 1999 novel *The Blackwater Lightship*, short-listed for the Booker prize and a landmark text, the first mainstream Irish AIDS narrative.[45] In the light of these changes, in the final chapter of this study I will discuss the ways in which these fictional texts reflected the Ireland of the twenty-first century and examine the imaginings of Wilde in the new century, a fusing of Oscar the Rebel with the idea of Wilde the Queer hero.

7. Wilde in the twenty-first century: 2000–2010

At the beginning of this decade, in the centenary year of Wilde's death in December 2000, President Mary MacAleese visited a centenary exhibition about Wilde in the British Library. *The Irish Times* noted that her speech was 'reflecting on a "hesitancy" of ownership of Wilde in Ireland and Britain. With a refreshing honesty, Mrs MacAleese said that on the anniversary of his death, Ireland was "justly, joyfully" celebrating his work and life but in the past, as she points out, with a refreshing honesty, "Irish people have sometimes been unsure how to regard him".'[1] Ireland was still a little unsure of Wilde as, throughout the first decade of the twenty-first century, both gay and straight Irish culture sought to appropriate Wilde as a potent symbol of affirmation and a signal for a reinvented Irish cultural modernity. In this final chapter, I want to consider fictive and scholarly versions of Wilde in the new century and focus in particular on the ways in which Irish gay writers have reconfigured Wilde. With new lgbt (lesbian gay bisexual transgender) and queer political and artistic Irish identities developing during this decade, a more expansive representation of the homoerotic was now possible, as can be seen in the fictions of Tóibín, Donoghue and O'Neill.

Wilde's cultural presence continued to be reformulated as the new century opened and progressed as Ireland grew wealthier and more self-consciously modernised. Witness also the logo of the Dublin Gay Theatre Festival, which began in 2004, where Wilde is a central figure for the festival, the symbol of a contemporary gay forum. In 2007, in line with their policy of naming their ferries for Irish literary figures, Irish Ferries christened its most recently acquired luxury cruise ship, which sails between Ireland and France, the *Oscar Wilde*. Enniskillen was also busy revising its former unease with one of Portora's most famous students when the Oscar Wilde Festival was launched in 2002. The following year, on 13 February 2003, a plaque was unveiled by the Parliamentary Under-Secretary of State Angela Smith MP and her speech was reported in a news release from her department:

> The Minister was speaking at Portora Royal School, Enniskillen, where she was unveiling a blue historical plaque, provided by the Ulster Historical Society, to celebrate the seven years Oscar Wilde

spent at the School before continuing his education at Trinity College, Dublin and Magdalen College, Oxford. Angela Smith said: 'As an avid reader of the works of Oscar Wilde, I am delighted, and indeed honoured, to have been invited to perform this unveiling ceremony at the opening of the second Oscar Wilde Festival in Enniskillen. Portora Royal School is a very appropriate location for such a commemorative plaque since Oscar Wilde spent his formative years here and it is said that his fairy tale, The Happy Prince, may have been inspired by the Cole Monument in the Fort Hill Pleasure Grounds. Of course, he went on to become one of Portora's best known former pupils and one of the greatest writers these islands have ever produced.'[2]

This open-hearted and unequivocal embracing of Wilde contrasts sharply with the earlier denials of Wilde in Portora. Two publications came from this Oscar Wilde Festival, both by Heather White, Wilde Fire and A Wilde Family,[3] with no mention of Wilde's homosexuality in either.

Critical thinking on Wilde the gay Irishman continued but in a much more fruitful manner than the above evasions. In 2003 Eiléan Ní Chuilleanáin published an edited collection called The Wilde Legacy,[4] the proceedings of a conference held in Trinity College Dublin in November 2000 to mark the hundredth anniversary of Wilde's death. In 1997 Trinity College set up the Oscar Wilde Centre for Irish Writing and this conference was held under its auspices, because now, as the editor noted, 'The college wished to commemorate and claim a famous former student'.[5] The conference focused on the whole Wilde family because, again in the words of Ní Chuilleanáin, previous studies of the family often reflected 'a deliberate limitation of the scope of their personalities'.[6] In the introduction to the book of the conference proceedings, the editor noted that, for her own mother, the novelist Eilís Dillon, and for many of her social class, Wilde had achieved the status of a martyr to the Irish Catholic nationalists of the 1930s.[7] Much of this book concentrates on the achievements and scholarship of Sir William and Speranza, but two contributors, Lucy McDiarmid and Alan Sinfield, open up new debates in relation to Wilde's place in Irish Republican iconography and also, for the first time, on Wilde's homosexuality as it was perceived in Ireland.

In her essay, Lucy McDiarmid quotes Tom Paulin's assertion that:

> [Wilde's] mother was a leading Irish nationalist poet so really he was programmed to take the trajectory that is part of the culture and that is to end up in the dock, be sentenced, taken to jail, make a brilliant series of speeches from the dock, and to be remembered as a martyr. Now he is a great gay martyr but he is following also the trajectory of so many Irish republicans.[8]

Her counter-argument is that Wilde never used the established language of the nineteenth-century Irish patriot and, in particular, never sought death or martyrdom in the interests of his cause, his legal challenge to Queensberry. In place of this notion of Wilde the Irish rebel, McDiarmid interprets Wilde as part of another tradition of what she calls 'oppositional celebrities',[9] like Byron and others who sought to disrupt the certainties and conformities of middle-class and upper-class society with a transgressive aesthetic. In a witty phrase, McDiarmid argues that for Wilde 'it's not Tiocfaidh ár lár but épater le bourgeois'.[10] Also she suggests that Wilde was deploying a late-Victorian ideology of Hellenistic (and homoerotic) art to justify and defend his same-sex activities as platonic and never resorted to an Irish Republican genealogy or language as a resistance to blame and censure. She argues that, unlike Wilde and other oppositional celebrities, Irish rebels were sexual conformists, conservative and well behaved in terms of their domestic lives. Irish nationalism and sexual rebellion were, it seems, incompatible. She makes the shrewd observation that it was the Mary Travers libel case and not the Charles Gavan Duffy trial that offered Wilde an exemplar of his family's relationship with the law. McDiarmid offers as a concluding argument that 'Slowly, gradually, after his release, Wilde began to speak with a different consciousness of the trial's meaning. Retrospectively, he shaped his experiences to fit the religious paradigm from which the Irish paradigm takes it shape: "I shall now live as the Infamous St Oscar of Oxford, Poet and Martyr", he wrote to Robbie Ross in 1898.'[11] McDiarmid's essay marks a new engagement with the idea of Wilde the Irishman, a nuance beyond the mere acceptance of his Republican credentials.

Alan Sinfield's essay '"I See It Is My *Name* that Terrifies": Wilde in the Twentieth Century' is the sole contribution to this collection that considers public perceptions around the notion of Wilde's homosexuality. He argues that the name and the persona 'Oscar Wilde' became the public idea of what a queer or disruptively gay man was in England and the USA: 'They didn't recognise Wilde as a homosexual because they didn't know what that unnamed creation looked like. They didn't know, as we do now, that he looked like Oscar Wilde.'[12] Sinfield goes on to suggest: 'How far and in what ways the dissemination of the Wildean queer images might apply to Ireland needs a lot more investigation.'[13] It is true that the idea of Wilde as 'authentically' Irishness was always contentious, but, when he was finally reclaimed in the 1980s and 1990s, what happens to representations of his sexual otherness? Sinfield argues that all references to his homosexuality disappear. 'For how can Wilde's Irish be addressed without including his queerness? The answer is: more readily than might have been supposed . . . Queerness is English to the point where even an Irish school that cultivated English principles could not have kindled it.'[14] Sinfield cites the fact that Coakley only mentions Wilde's sexuality on the eve of the trials, right at the end of his book, and that Richard Pine sees his queerness as Oxford derived, as does Denis Donoghue and Terry Eagleton too. In this new 1980s version of Wilde the Irishman, his homosexuality becomes the fault of a British upper-class imperialist system and the degenerate sexual perversion at its core. McCormack, Heaney and Kiberd, in Sinfield's view, allow Wilde's homosexuality, as it were, to 'fade into a general post-modern indeterminacy'[15] and, in particular, Kiberd's view of Wilde's sexuality as a kind of generalised androgyny draws the response from Sinfield that Wilde 'liked boys to the point where he risked destruction: he did, at a common sense level, rely on a divide between male and female'.[16]

Sinfield makes the point about mac Líammóir that he 'didn't only want to be a queer on the Wildean model; he wanted to be Irish'[17] and goes on to argue that mac Líammóir 'signals the affinity under the name of Wilde, of queerness and Irishness. What we would like to know now is whether other, less famous Irishmen presented themselves in Wildean manner, and how their contemporaries regarded them.'[18] For Sinfield, mac Líammóir is the true gay radical in his own self-presentation and in his affinity with Wilde: 'The opportunity mac Líammóir was seeking to embody is for Ireland to share with England that substantive segment of gay history which Wilde had been made to designate . . . Camp style was sufficiently like Irish style, in other words, to enable Wilde to pass . . . The Wildean queer, as mac Líammóir found in his own life, may be at home in Dublin.'[19] Sinfield ends his essay with the argument that

> It is not queerness that is peculiarly English, then, as seems to be the view of some of the commentators I discussed earlier, but a stodgy and irrational phobia about queerness; whereas revolutionary Ireland can incorporate dissident sexuality into its epic project . . . If the Wildean model of the queer man is a rightful part of Irish inheritance, that does not mean that this is what Irish gays must be like. To the contrary, as in England, the Wildean legacy is there to be recovered, contested and negotiated. It is a tool for thinking with, not an identity to be adopted.[20]

Sinfield's analysis of Wilde's gay Irishness is a distinctive, original one in contemporary critical readings of Wilde and is paralleled, in terms of creative representations of Wilde, by the writings of Colm Tóibín and Jamie O'Neill.

Apart from these essay collections or book chapters, full-length studies of Wilde in Irish studies are few, but Jarlath Killeen's *The Faiths of Oscar Wilde* (2005) takes a new approach to Wilde and considers the influence of Irish Catholicism on Wilde: 'The writings of Oscar Wilde can fruitfully be analysed as expressive of an Irish Catholic heritage.'[21] Killeen is reclaiming him for contemporary Irish studies: 'In the history of criticism devoted to Wilde, however, up to the 1990s, the Irish cultural milieu in which he grew up was, if anything, de-emphasised, or read simply as biographical background . . . Deane argues that Wilde made too many compromises with English literary convention to be considered a truly Irish figure.'[22] Killeen exempts Kiberd, who recognised that Wilde was continuing his own parents' nationalist project of subverting and undermining British society, but he does criticise Eagleton, Pine, Coakley and others for reclaiming Wilde as Irish but Protestant Irish. Killeen's thesis is that Wilde was, in fact and in faith, a true Irish Catholic, not just attracted to the homoeroticised Catholic aesthetic of 'bells and smells' but to its core spiritual beliefs. Shane Leslie had interpreted Wilde's homosexuality as the obstacle to his conversion to Catholicism, and his writings as a block on the way to his salvation. Instead, Killeen argues that Wilde's homosexuality meant that, up to the 1960s in Ireland, his writings were branded as the product of deviancy or of tragic victimhood. After the 1960s, Killeen suggests, Wilde was gradually seen as transgressive and subversive of colonisation, but this has meant that his sincere interest in Catholicism was now dismissed by Irish critics as trivial or, worse, English. Killeen puts forward the novel argument that Wilde's Catholicism was both Irish in origin and sincere in intent and a fruitful part of his sexuality. Thus he can interpret Wilde's Irishness and Catholicism as a creative dynamic between the hegemonic and the subversive.

Killeen's central thesis is that the dynamic between Wilde's Catholicism and his Irishness is vital and that Catholicism was his secret life. To expound this view of Wilde, Killeen reads various Wildean texts in terms of an Irish tradition, not at all in the conventional sense of a Republican tradition but rather in terms of a religious one: 'Salome needs to be rooted in the Ireland of the nineteenth century and particularly the religious controversies that animated the debates between second reformation Protestant Evangelicals and Catholics in poverty-stricken regions during the Irish Famine.'[23] He goes on, 'In my discussion, I have placed *Salome* in both a biographical (Evangelical) and a national context and demonstrated that the writings of his parents remain basic for interpretations of his play . . . Taken together, *The Portrait of Mr WH* and *Salome* reinterpret the Gospel stories through the folk-Catholic version of the story found in the West of Ireland.'[24]

Killeen extends his reading of the Wildean texts as closet Irish Catholic tales by suggesting that *The Picture of Dorian Gray* is a Gothic decadent text and thus anti-realist, anti-English and anti-colonial. He argues that

> Colonialism used Irish folk-Catholicism as an example of how back-
> ward Ireland was, how lost in time the Irish people were. From a
> colonial point of view, depicting the Irish as a charmingly primitive
> people justified depriving them of the means of self-government.
> Wilde's novel is an attempt to preserve Irish folk-Catholicism from
> being overwhelmed by such threats and used as an instrument in fur-
> thering the colonial mission.[25]

Wilde's central protagonist, Dorian, thus stands in for the uncivilised Irish, tamed, civilised, seduced and betrayed by the Englishmen Lord Henry and Basil: 'Through the fate of Dorian, Wilde demonstrates the dangers to Ireland when its anti-mimetic traditions are translated into a commodity rather than left as a living tradition.'[26] Killeen's study is a remarkable one, fluently argued and original.

In a later study, *The Fairy Tales of Oscar Wilde* (2007), Killeen con-
tinues his engagement with Wilde from within contemporary Irish studies by focusing on his two collections *The Happy Prince and Other Tales* (1888) and *A House of Pomegranates* (1891). In this study, Killeen argues that Ireland is the source of inspiration for the fairy tales, and a recent critical desire to separate them from Wilde's other works arises from the perception of them as an unwanted, conservative side to his creativity. Fairy tales are seen as traditionally conservative, a strategy by which the middle class socialised and made conformist their children, while folk tales are seen as subversive, giving hope of escape to submerged communities. Killeen embraces this dichotomy by suggesting that 'the fairy tales should be read as containing both conservative and subversive energies, and that they allow us to see Wilde himself as dis-
playing the qualities of a conservative as well as a radical writer. I contend that the fairy tales should be read in relation to that field of force from which Wilde drew much of his creative energies – Ireland – and that when placed in this context the strange, often disturbing, qualities of the stories begin to make sense. In re-situating these fairy tales in the complex nexus of theological, political, social and national concerns of late-nineteenth-century, some of the difficulties critics have encoun-
tered will, hopefully, be removed'.[27]

Killeen sees the Irishness of these tales as crucial, particularly as a manifestation of Wilde's sincere and Irish-inspired Catholicism: 'I am suggesting that recognising the Irishness of these tales and their folk-
Catholic elements helps to banish some of the critical mystery that adheres to them.'[28] In his concluding argument, Killeen draws a useful

parallel with encoded elements of race. 'As queer theorists are looking for signs of Wilde's sexuality in quasi-heterosexual texts like *The Importance of Being Earnest*, we have to realise that another culture saturated in the concept of the secret symbol in the nineteenth century was Catholicism.'[29]

This remaking of Wilde in critical terms is paralleled on the stage. Tom Kilroy returned to the figure of Wilde in 2004 with his unperformed play *My Scandalous Life*, an excellent dramatic monologue with Alfred Douglas as the central figure. This is a rare text in the Wildean canon, a play sympathetic to Bosie and a resituating of Bosie within a tragic domestic world, with his son Raymond in a state of mental disturbance. As with the earlier play about Constance Wilde, this work re-examines the myths around Wilde and establishes a real sense of respect and sympathy for Bosie and for his relationship with Wilde. Set in England in 1944, the year before his death, in this play Douglas meditates on his own life after the trials, his various court cases, his marriage, the tragic mental illness of his only son and the poisonous legacy of his turbulent association with Wilde – 'Oscar Wilde, did you say? That's all you lot ever ask about.'[30] Douglas, in this account, is devious, self-deceiving and filled with hatred and rancour, especially against Robert Ross, but Kilroy imagines that Douglas finally managed to achieve a kind of wisdom in spite of his paranoia and anger, an understanding of the link between himself and Wilde. This crucial moment of insight into the bond between Wilde and Douglas is rare in depictions of their fatal association and worth noting. At one point in the play, Douglas is questioned by one of his young friends about *De Profundis* and Wilde's motivation in writing such a cruel and relentless indictment of the man he loved: '"Why," he asked eventually, "why had Oscar Wilde written that terrible letter about me when he was in prison when he and I clearly loved one another to the end? Oh innocence! Innocence!" I found the look on the boy's face unbearable. He wanted some answer but was terrified that the answer would destroy some belief which he held dear.'[31] Kilroy imagines Douglas replying in terms that suggest plausibility and a dignified acknowledgement of the enduring connection between the two men.

> I told him that prison was about failure . . . that at the very heart of existence is this well of failure and that to look into this black pool was to cleanse oneself, forever, of all illusion, about others, about oneself. How could I explain that Oscar, too, had looked into this pit and then wrote that terrible letter about me? How could I explain that that was the reason, too, why I could forgive him? You see, we had both become truth-tellers, able to cut through deception, especially our own self-deception.[32]

This representation of a real emotional connection between Bosie and Wilde echoes Kilroy's earlier sense of a connection between Constance and Wilde and marks an advance in the ways in which Wilde's downfall is portrayed, not as a sin or a tragedy but more as a complex series of interconnected relationships. The sympathetic sense of a connection between Wilde and Bosie is also a feature of the critical writings of Colm Tóibín, and Tóibín's writings are themselves informed by wider trends and possiblities within current Irish gay writing, where Wilde can now be reclaimed as both Irish and 'queer'. In a society where artists can identify themselves as gay, their writings become more complex, as Gregory Woods writes, 'Even given the effects of homophobia on the production, distribution and evaluation of texts, we are increasingly in charge of our own culture. We have our own requirements and set our own standards thereby.'[33] Not surprisingly, gay theorists and cultural commentators have been reclaiming Wilde as queer radical and to good effect. Wilde has long been a figure of importance for lesbian and gay theorists outside Ireland like Ed Cohen, Neil Bartlett, Alan Sinfield, Eve Kosofsky Sedgewick, Jonathan Dollimore and Joseph Bristow but, in the past ten years, Irish gay writers have been making Wilde not only queer but Irish. The cultural critic and journalist Dermod Moore, in his book *Diary of a Man* (2005), writes:

> The great actor, Micheál mac Líammóir was buried with a green carnation on his coffin in '78 and all the papers mentioned Hilton Edwards at the funeral, in a different way than normal. But no one made it explicit that these eminent men of the theatre were partners. There were vague references to Oscar Wilde – but there seemed to be something very English about the vice of homosexuality, the prison sentences and the theatricality of it. Not Irish.[34]

What about Queer Wilde for Ireland in the twenty-first century? Joyce's interpretation of Wildean sin as redemptive and enabling was prescient in that it is now relocated in the works of contemporary gay writers like Tóibín and O'Neill, at a time when queer Irishness has been identified as possible and visible. Thus Wilde figured as both queer and rebel.

In his own lifetime, Wilde was seen as decadent and now this decadence has been reinterpreted as queer. Matthew Sturgis in his study *Passionate Attitudes* argues that 'although decadence in England during the 1890s never quite managed to refine itself into a movement, it did create a pungent and distinctive flavour'[35] and sees 'distrust of Victorian confidence in society's common aims and standards, both artistic and moral: belief in the essential loneliness of the individual's consciousness and the consolation of aesthetic impressions; belief too in art's superiority to nature – and to life'.[36] Wilde embodied many of these qualities, in a kind of proto-queerness, and so when he was brought to trial, his connections with French decadent writing became a focus for attack. Queer studies has become a vital part of Irish literary and cultural discourse in the last ten years and Anne Mulhall, in her discussion of contemporary Irish queer communality, notes that:

> 'Effeminacy' is invoked, via Ashis Nandy's psychosocial model of postcolonial 'hypermasculinity' as the emasculating effect of colonial subjection on the colonial male in particular. Robbed of agency, made the passive object of colonial surveillance and dehumanization, categorized as 'feminine', irrational, barbaric and unfit for self-government, the male subject and the nation-state after colonialism repeat the cycle of abuse. Disavowing his current or former abject state, the post-colonized man must assert his masculinity with increased force, and hence the punitive legal and social sanctions against homosexuality and the rigid curtailment of women's freedoms in the post-colonial nation-state.[37]

With a contemporary dismantling of this colonial and post-colonial fear of the effeminate, Wilde's sexual otherness can now be seen in tandem with his Irishness. In this instance, Annamarie Jagose's definition of queer is most useful where she suggests that 'Broadly speaking queer describes those gestures or analytical models which dramatise incoherencies in the allegedly stable relations between chromosomal sex, gender and sexual desire. Resisting that model of stability – which claims heterosexuality as its origins when it is more properly its effect – queer focuses on mismatches between sex, gender and desire.'[38] As well as linking with Wilde's earlier decadence, queerness resists models and discourses of stability like that of Irish nationalism and this resistance is made possible in Irish culture of the 2000s. In his introduction to his edited collection of plays, *Queer Notions*, in 2010, Fintan Walsh describes the time frame in which these queer plays were created in Ireland:

> Written and performed between 2000 and 2010, the pieces both challenge, but also strive to imagine alternative ways of being with others, and being in the world. The works are queer in so far as they explore tensions surrounding sexual difference in the broadest sense, in a manner that illuminates and interrogates issues that affect a wide range of people, including those who neither identify as Irish nor queer.[39]

The gap between Rebel Wilde and Queer Wilde can thus be fruitfully exploited.

In this section I want to consider Wilde as an emblematic figure in present day gay writing. Matt Cook has written that 'Both Wilde and

Wildean strategies were increasingly seen as ways of thinking about the constitution and malleability of homosexual identity in the 1880s and the 1890s and also as a means of self-invention, affirmation and endurance in the present.[40] Both Tóibín and O'Neill deploy the iconic figure of Wilde as a means of affirmation and endurance for a contemporary gay identity, and do so by fusing his nationalism with the potentially subversive nature of his sexual dissidence.

Interestingly, in this decade, novelists like Tóibín, O'Neill and Donoghue looked to the form of the historical novel to explore the complexities of lesbian and gay identity in the new century. For example, I would suggest that Donoghue, in *Life Mask*, published in 2004 and set in the years 1787 to 1797, uses her research on lesbian and gay history to draw a portrait of a homophobic society and of an earlier lesbian selfhood. Her central character is the real-life Anne Damer, sister of the Duchess of Richmond, well connected in Georgian aristocratic society and a sculptor of note. The novel examines Anne Damer's relationship with Eliza Farren, the Irish actress, and Lord Derby, the wealthy nobleman who aspires to marry the working woman Eliza Farren. The developing friendship between Anne Damer and the young actress abruptly ends when an anonymous poem is circulated and printed, hinting at Damer's sapphism. Interestingly this is Donoghue's most sustained examination of the effects of a public atmosphere of homophobia on a private life, seen in the conjunction between straight and lesbian desire. The Wildean parallels are clear in this story of panic and public scrutiny from a lesbian past and historical parallels are also drawn here with media hysteria in England at this time of revolution in France and contemporary North American pressure of public opinion and hysteria against same-sex passion in the wake of 9/11. (At one point, the phrase 'Homeland Security' is used by one of the eighteenth-century English news-sheets!) Because of the pressure of political turmoil from abroad, English aristocratic society is the focus for public attack and a faultline within this culture is the notion of same-sex desire between women, at a time when so-called 'tommys' or sapphists are ridiculed and attacked. The life mask is the mask of the closet and, when Anne Damer confronts her private and public demons, she realises that the slander is true and claims the name of sapphist for herself, finding a life-long partnership with Mary Berry. Donoghue uses her historical novel to suggest a means of transcending homophobic panic.

Novels from the past can destabilise the present. In Jamie O'Neill's 2002 novel *At Swim, Two Boys*, a narrative of homoerotic love and romance set around the Easter Rising of 1916, the figure of Oscar Wilde functions as both iconic queer and also symbol of patriotic rebellion, and each version of Wilde empowers and fuses with the other. One of the central characters, Anthony MacMurrough, is directly figured as a Wildean transgressor, as he has also been imprisoned for gross indecency and has served the full sentence of two years' hard labour. MacMurrough constantly invokes the shade of the now dead, queer Wilde at this time of nationalist agitation. At one point, MacMurrough is on a tour of Dublin with his aunt, a tour given by a nationalist Irish priest. They arrive in Merrion Square. '"I don't believe I know", the priest remarked, "any patriot associated with Merrion Square".'[41] MacMurrough, to annoy his aunt, intervenes and tells the priest:

> 'There was one Irishman associated with Merrion Square,' he said. 'Yes, the English put him on trial.'
> 'It was ever the way,' the priest complacently affirmed.
> 'Three trials, in fact. On the first he had the wit to proclaim, I am the prosecutor in this case!'
> 'I see, yes, very good. For all his country's wrongs.'
> 'I need hardly tell you, Father Taylor, of the desertion by his friends, of witnesses bullied and corrupted, of the agitation against him got up by the newspapers.'
> 'It was ever the Saxon sneaking way' . . .
> 'His conviction was inevitable. But from the dock he gave a cele-brated speech that defied to the heavens the traductions of his adversaries.'
> 'A speech from the dock! I have heard it said, and have said it myself; the speech from the dock is the only truly Irish drama. Three patriots may not gather but a rendition of Emmet or of Tone will edify the occasion. It is a form peculiarly suited to the Irish temperament. And what did this speech from the dock say?'
> 'The jury was unmoved, the judge called for order but still the gallery cheered.'[42]

The priest never finds out the name of this great Irish patriot. MacMurrough's aunt intervenes before Wilde's unmentionable name can be mentioned, but the whole Irish patriot reincarnation of Wilde is being teased and undermined by O'Neill. MacMurrough's aunt reproves him:

> 'Are you really so lunatic . . . that you were about to give Oscar Wilde's name to the parish curate?' . . .
> 'Well,' said MacMurrough, 'and was he not an Irishman? And did his speech not bring the gallery to its feet?'
> 'You refer to the eulogium on illicit love?'
> 'The love that dares not speak its name.'
> 'Its name,' she said, 'is buggery. Any soul in the three kingdoms might have told him.'[43]

In this tale of love between Irish men in time of war, the image of Wilde presides, even to a point of parody and farce, when, at one point, MacMurrough rescues a man in difficulty swimming in Dublin Bay and, on discovering that he has actually rescued Edward Carson, insists on giving him a full-on kiss, just to revenge himself for Wilde's sake. At another point, the Irish patriot Tom Kettle, here presented as an old schoolfriend of MacMurrough, asks, appalled, when confronted with MacMurrough's homosexuality, "'Dammit, MacMurrough, are you telling me that you are an unspeakable of the Oscar Wilde sort?' 'If you mean, am I Irish, the answer is yes.'"[44] For O'Neill, as for Joyce, another direct influence on this novel, the figure of Wilde can be deployed as an empowering prophet of sin. In a perceptive review of the novel, David Halperin argues that

> One of O'Neill's most breathtaking accomplishments in *At Swim, Two Boys* is to cross the codes of Irish identity and gay identity, making each into a figure for the other, thereby producing at one stroke a gay genealogy of Irishness as well as a specifically Irish image of male homosexuality – a romantic vision of the gay male world as 'a nation of the heart' . . . O'Neill's novel deliberately takes its readers back to the pivotal era when gayness and Irishness alike were under vigorous construction . . . Little wonder, then, that the plot of *At Swim, Two Boys* hurtles relentlessly towards Easter 1916: both Irish nationalism and queer nationalism locate their mythological origins in an urban riot. Impertinent as it might seem to claim the Irish Rebellion as a prototype of Stonewall, O'Neill – who is not above making obscene puns on Ireland's 'rising' – does finally invite us to view Stonewall as a latter-day gay replica of Easter 1916.[45]

As Halperin suggests, the novel fuses the two possible kinds of Irish Wilde and its queerness destablises the heretofore heteronormativity of Irish Republican discourse.

The novelist Colm Tóibín also constructs Wilde as an Irish gay icon, an empowering presence in contemporary Irish writing, in his essay on Wilde in *Love in a Dark Time: Gay Lives from Wilde to Almodovar* (2002). In this collection, Tóibín links his own recognition of himself as a gay man with his reclaiming of Wilde as a crucial point of reference. His essay on Wilde is perhaps the most direct account of the importance of Wilde's sexuality from a contemporary Irish gay literary and cultural perspective and he opens with the question: 'Why should it matter? It matters because as gay readers and writers become more visible and confident, and gay politics more settled and serious, gay history becomes a vital element in gay identity, just as Irish history does in Ireland, or Jewish history amongst Jewish people.'[46] 'The gay past is not pure (as the Irish past can often seem too pure); it is duplicitous and slippy.'[47] Tóibín makes the link between the unhappy, despairing gay writing of the past and unhappy Irish domestic writing, but, unusually for an Irish commentator writing on Wilde, he cites Sir William as the crucial parental influence that made Wilde decide to prosecute Queensberry. 'The Wildes were part of a small breed of Irish Protestants . . . Their addiction to the cause of Irish freedom gave them an edge, lifted them out of their own circumstances and gave them astonishing individuality, and independence of mind.'[48] Tóibín records Wilde's respect for Speranza, much needed after all the sneering or grotesque accounts of his mother that appeared in earlier Irish biographies of Wilde: 'In all of Oscar Wilde's letters in which he refers to his mother, there is not one word of mockery or disloyalty. Mostly he refers to her not as his mother but as Lady Wilde.'[49] He also stresses that all grotesque accounts of Speranza happen after Wilde's trials and disgrace and that before 1895 all the contemporary accounts of her are respectful and admiring, her reputation as a writer suffering as a consequence of his downfall.

Tóibín is refreshingly perceptive on the idea of how gay men approach sexual relationships, using Wilde and Douglas as his exemplars, and addresses the assumptions of earlier biographers:

> [quoting Richard Ellmann] 'Since neither Wilde nor Douglas practised or expected sexual fidelity, money was the stamp and seal of their love.' That last sentence, so full of judgement and certainty, shows us perhaps more about Ellmann than it does about Wilde or Douglas. It suggests that 'since' they were not faithful to each other, they could not properly love each other; he suggests that 'since' this is the case, then the stamp and seal of their love would have to be something profane and abject and wrong. It is much more likely that the stamp and seal of their love came from their enormous attraction to each other, their need for each other, and something difficult to define and explain which is at the core of homosexual experience in the era before gay liberation and perhaps to some extent, in the era afterwards.[50]

Unlike Ellmann and many other Wildean biographers, Tóibín takes the relationship between Bosie and Wilde seriously and treats their relationship with a real respect for its authentic emotional bonding:

> In most societies, most gay people go through adolescence believing that the fulfilment of physical desire would not be matched by emotional attachment. For straight people, the eventual matching of the two is part of the deal, a happy aspect of normality. But if this occurs for gay people, it is capable of taking on an extraordinarily powerful emotional force, and the resulting attachment, even if the physical

part fizzles out, or even if the relationship makes no sense to the outside world, is likely to be fierce and enduring ... This, more likely, was the stamp and seal of the love between Oscar Wilde and Alfred Douglas.[51]

As Tóibín puts it: 'The personal became political because an Irishman in London pushed his luck.'[52]

For Tóibín and Donoghue, the past is a metaphor for the present, a means by which the present can be re-evaluated. For Colm Tóibín, the homoerotic makes a belated appearance in his fiction. In his earlier novels, *The South* and *The Heather Blazing*, the imaginative context is firmly normative and heterosexual and it is only with his third novel, *The Story of the Night*, that a homoerotic narrative is introduced, albeit displaced on to a South American setting. Finally, in conjunction with his public self-identification as gay, Tóibín published his first novel where a contemporary Irish gay identity is represented. However, I would argue that in *The Blackwater Lightship* the homoerotic vanishes as a legitimised gay identity emerges from Irish law. In his novel *The Master* (2004), as with the O'Neill novel, Wilde has a crucial symbolic role, the dangerous 'other' figure for the closeted and cautious Henry James, the master of the title. The turning point in James's life in London comes in April and May 1895 during the Wilde trials. Wilde obsesses James, a nightmare counterpart, a dreaded anti-self, publicly exposed and forced to defend his homosexuality in a courtroom, and, as can be seen in this excerpt, Tóibín aligns Wilde's dangerous sexuality with his national identity:

> Everything about Wilde, from the moment Henry had first seen him, even when he had met him in Washington in the house of Clover Adams, suggested deep levels and layers of hiddenness ... He remembered something vague being told to him about Wilde's parents, his mother's madness, or her revolutionary spirit, or both, and his father's philandering or perhaps, indeed, his revolutionary spirit. Ireland, he supposed, was too small for someone like Wilde, yet he had always carried a threat of Ireland with him.[53]

James is fascinated and also terrified by Wilde and by any supposed connection that might be made between the two men. (James, like Wilde, was of Irish Protestant stock but James keeps his Irish ancestry quiet.) The lesson of Wilde's disgrace drives James most decisively back into further closeted self-denial, but, by implication, the figure of Wilde acts as a kind of destabilising force within the novel, the subversive Irishman willing to confront public homophobia, a sexual rebel in a way that the repressed James can never emulate.

The story of Wilde filled Henry's days now. He read whatever came into print about the case and waited for news. He wrote to William about the trial, making clear that he had no respect for Wilde; he disliked both his work and his activities on the stage of London society. Wilde, he insisted, had never been interesting to him, but now, as Wilde threw caution away and seemed ready to make himself into a public martyr, the Irish playwright began to interest him enormously.[54]

Wilde becomes another self for James, a liberated, visible, Irish queer man, everything that fascinated and also repelled him, and this episode is seen as crucial in the lifelong closetry and sexual timidity of the novelist. In Tóibín's account, Wilde frightens James into the closet for ever. Oscar Wilde's very public trials, disgrace and downfall, observed in London in April 1895 with some horror by James, has particular implications for James's own sense of himself as a gay man.

In this beautifully crafted novel, Tóibín builds up slowly and carefully James's evolving attitude towards his own sexuality in his representations of the male body. Early on in the novel the young James shares a bed with Oliver Wendell Holmes and watches him undress. 'For a second, as his friend remained still, he could have been a statue of a young man, tall and muscular. As Henry studied him, he forgot his moustache and his craggy features.'[55] Later, describing the two men in bed, Tóibín suggests an unspoken moment of sexual consummation, the only such moment in James's life.

As they lay back to back, he could feel the carefully tensed presence against him. He waited, knowing that it was inevitable that Holmes would turn, inevitable that something would occur to break this silent, deadlocked game they were playing. Holmes, he felt, was as consciously involved as he was in what might happen. He was not surprised then when Holmes turned and cupped him with his body and placed one hand against his back and another against his shoulder.[56]

During the course of the narrative and during James's long friendship with Holmes, this moment is spoken about and never acknowledged. With Wilde as a warning and because of late-Victorian suspicions around the homoerotic, James firmly represses his homosexuality. Yet his viewing of the male body as an object of desire and potential aesthetic source is stressed again and again.

Voyeuristic homoerotic desire rather than sexual consummation becomes the focus for James's real interest, and this unfulfilled desire, it is implied, enriches James's writing while impoverishing his erotic life. He controls any expression of his sexuality most carefully, for example in the case of his attraction towards his Irish servant Hammond and also his interest in the younger sculptor Hendrick Anderson. Anderson comes to stay at Lamb House, but although James desires him he makes no declaration or move and instead listens to him undressing in the next room:

> As the floorboards creaked under Anderson's feet, Henry imagined his friend undressing, removing his jacket and tie. And then he heard only silence as perhaps Anderson sat on the bed to remove his shoes and socks . . . He wondered if he would not remove his trousers and his underwear and stand naked studying himself in the mirror, looking at how the sun had marked his neck, observing how strong he was, staring at the blue of his own eyes, not making a sound.[57]

James succeeds in controlling any outward interest or surveillance of his sexuality in a society where all sexual liaisons are under scrutiny. James's life is made subservient to his art, and his repression, it is implied, serves his fiction well, the implication being that a life spent writing such books was a life worth living, even at the cost of sexual self-realisation. Tóibín allows us to read James's bravery as a writer as the sole act of defiance in his closeted life. At the end of the novel James is left alone and happy in Lamb House, clear that he has lived his life as an observer and not as a participant, to the detriment of his personal life but greatly to the advantage of his novel-making. What is Tóibín saying about his own fiction in his return to the historical-novel form, his struggle to refocus his sense of moving in from the margins? Perhaps it is that liminality is almost always crucial to any expression of the homoerotic in literary discourse, and the past, for him, is the only arena in which to remake notions of the homoerotic for the present. Tóibín has written that 'the idea that gay writing has a tendency to deal with the tragic and the unfulfilled, a tendency which Forster and writers after Stonewall sought to counteract, has echoes in Irish writing . . . This truth may change, of course, as gay lives change and Ireland changes.'[58]

An all-male production of *The Importance of Being Earnest* was staged at the Abbey Theatre in 2005, a production which staged the play itself in the last year of Wilde's own life in Paris. In the play Wilde takes various roles and the French rent boys take the parts of the main characters, thus bringing the gay subtext to the fore. The conjunction of Wilde's Irishness and the mainstream nature of his subversive sexuality are made plain in an essay in *The Irish Times* on 27 July 2005 called 'A Peek through Oscar's Glasses', which incorporated an interview with the director:[59]

> Conall Morrison's all-male *The Importance of Being Earnest* at the Abbey Theatre bravely places Oscar Wilde as a character in the play;

> Conall Morrison knows that directing *The Importance of Being Earnest* for the Abbey Theatre this month will be a challenge . . . Morrison sees it as a way to bring out the serious and courageous questions that Wilde's play, cloaked in glittering comedy, dared to ask . . . But is Morrison wary that the subtlety of the play could be swallowed up in camp? 'Firstly, I'm very happy to reap any comic rewards,' he smiles. 'But with the prologue, the audience will have seen the real face of Oscar's engagement with a gay existence . . . And if you think of Oscar casting men in these roles, look at Hollywood and how many stars still cannot come out of the closet. It's far from won. Far from won.'[60]

In this production, the same actor, Alan Stanford, played Wilde in the preface to the play and then took the part of Lady Bracknell and of the servant Lane (breaking down barriers of gender and class), and men play Cecily and Gwendolen and Ms Prism. The play was well received – perhaps because Morrison's production stayed safely within gender divisions, with little or no physical contact between the men. Rather, there was an emphasis on containing any potential sexual subtexts within the play, thus creating little or no disturbance for its Dublin audience, who were happy to see Wilde updated and made clearly queer.

To conclude, Wilde is a key figure in the first scholarly account of Irish lesbian and gay history, Brian Lacey's 2008 *Terrible Queer Creatures*.[61] In this wide-ranging historical and cultural account of lesbian and gay figures in Irish history, Wilde is, unsurprisingly, the key figure on the book cover and inside. Indeed, Lacey opens his book with the moment where Queensberry leaves his insulting card for Wilde at the Albemarle, thus initiating the trials and Wilde's downfall, and makes explicit the reclamation of Wilde as a contemporary gay icon for twenty-first-century Ireland: 'Apart from his fame as a writer and wit, Wilde has every right to be remembered as a gay martyr and hero. Apart from other things, he did not run away from the charges made against him.'[62]

Conclusion

The transformation of Ireland in the last thirty-five years or so, as I have outlined, also meant a transformation in the way in which Ireland viewed Oscar Wilde. There are many reasons for this: the end of Catholic control of public morality; the decriminalisation of male homosexuality and the emergence of a confident gay visibility; the influence of European law, and the wealth of the Celtic Tiger economy. Wilde, the celebrated wit and gay martyr, thus became an easily accessible icon for the modernisation and liberalism of Ireland in the twenty-first century, a signifier for the wholesale rejection of the insularity and perceived narrow-mindedness of the first sixty years of the new Irish state. Wilde's gayness, first recognised and affirmed by scholars outside of Irish intellectual life, has now become part of his public persona within Ireland, and it is linked to an apparent acceptance and liberalism towards contemporary Irish lesbians and gays. The surface nature of that acceptance and liberalism is evident in current debates over same-sex unions and family rights, and, in the same way, this contemporary reconstruction of Wilde the proud gay Irishman is equally fragile and unreflective.

I began by suggesting that Wilde was a shadow within Irish cultural discourse in his lifetime and immediately afterwards, to some in Ireland an emblem of subversion against Britain, sometimes a covert sign of sexual difference. Thus Wilde's shadow in Ireland has been altered and remade time and again by the changing cultural perceptions of homosexuality and also of sectarian identity. Wilde was now a silence, or a shape around a silence. Latterly it seems to me that Wilde has moved from shadow and silence and has become a mirror in which he is made to reflect the identity, class, gender and politics of each of his 'interpreters' in Ireland, those writers and critics who engage with his work. I would argue that, in the twentieth century, Irish Protestant writers and Irish gay writers clearly find much in Wilde with which to identify, particularly as a way of circumventing their own sense of cultural marginality within the new Ireland. Wilde, more than any other writer, lends himself to constant reinventions, because of the playful, subversive performative nature of his writings and his dramas. Modern Ireland, like many other postcolonial countries, is subject to endless self-scrutiny and cultural self-fashioning. Thus, Oscar's shadow, or mirror, like modern Irish cultural identity itself, reveals more of each historical moment than it does of Wilde himself. For Ireland, Wilde has been one of its clearest mirrors in the search for selfhood.

To conclude, I want to refer to a moment in Irish public discourse that highlights continuing ambivalent public perceptions around Wilde in contemporary Ireland. At the end of this decade, when it seems as if a queer Wilde has been recovered, another moment of public unease surfaced when a proposal to rename Merrion Square Park as Oscar Wilde Gardens was rejected by Dublin City Council. (The park, the site of the Wilde statue, had officially been called Archbishop Ryan Park, but this name was dropped in light of revelations about clerical abuse in the Dublin diocese.) In a letter to *The Irish Times* on Friday 14 May 2010, Ross Higgins wrote that he was 'deeply disappointed to hear of the decision of the councillors representing Dublin South East to recommend to the Dublin City Council that Archbishop Ryan Park be renamed Merrion Square Park rather than Oscar Wilde Gardens' ('Home News', 11 May). There was an extensive consultation process, with 567 submissions

('Home News', 7 May) received by the City Council, with 219 in favour of renaming the park Oscar Wilde Gardens and only 45 in favour of calling it Merrion Square Park. The park itself is the site of the only public memorial to Oscar Wilde and there is no public amenity in the city named after him, so this represented an opportunity to change this. I have heard it said that, since the park is commonly referred to as Merrion Square, why not make the name official? The problem is that names matter, and symbolism matters. After all, this is why the name of the park was being changed in the first place. The councillors, in overturning the clear response of the consultation process, were making a statement: 'that 110 years after his death Dublin should still be ashamed of one of its most gifted sons.[63] This attempt to change the name of the park failed, and the move to dissent from past clerical authority in the shape of Archbishop Ryan and align instead with the figure of Wilde as an icon of gay resistance was unsuccessful. Clearly, as I conclude this study in 2010, the problematic shadow of Oscar Wilde still troubles Irish public discourse.

Notes and references

1. IRELAND AND THE WILDE TRIALS: 1884–1907

1 Alan Sinfield, '"I See It Is My *Name* that Terrifies": Wilde in the Twentieth Century', in *The Wilde Legacy*, ed. Eileán Ní Chuilleanáin (Dublin: Four Courts, 2003), p. 145.

2 Alan Sinfield, *The Wilde Century: Effeminacy, Oscar Wilde and the Queer Moment* (London: Cassells, 1994).

3 I am grateful to Graham Allen for this interesting point.

4 Maria Luddy, *Prostitution and Irish Society, 1800–1940* (Cambridge: Cambridge University Press, 2008), p. 156.

5 St John Ervine, *Oscar Wilde: A Present Time Appraisal* (New York: Morrow, 1952), p. 35.

6 Lucy McDiarmid, *The Irish Art of Controversy* (Dublin: Lilliput, 2005), p. 205.

7 Jeffrey Weeks, *Sexuality* (London: Routledge, 2002), p. 33.

8 Matt Cook, *London and the Culture of Homosexuality, 1885–1914* (Cambridge: Cambridge University Press, 2003), p. 3. I am also indebted to Joseph Bristow's excellent work in this area of research.

9 Margot Norris, 'A Walk on the Wild(e) Side', in *Quare Joyce*, ed. Joseph Valente (Ann Arbor: University of Michigan Press, 1998), pp. 19–33.

10 H. Montgomery Hyde, *The Other Love: An Historical and Contemporary Survey of Homosexuality in Britain* (London: Heinemann, 1970), p. 133. I should like to thank Dr James H. Murphy, De Paul University, for generously sharing his forthcoming research publication on the Dublin Castle scandal.

11 León Ó Broin, *The Prime Informer* (London: Sidgwick & Jackson, 1971), p. 26.

12 Cook, *London and the Culture of Homosexuality*, p. 39.

13 The Queen versus Cornwall, Convicts References Files 1884, National Archives of Ireland, Dublin. I thank Ciarán Wallace for locating these materials in relation to the Dublin Castle scandal.

14 William O'Brien, *Evening Memories* (London: Maunsel, 1920), p. 31.

15 Ibid., p. 21.

16 Ó Broin, p. 28.

17 T.C. Breen, 'Loathsome, Impure and Revolting Crimes: The Dublin Scandals of 1884', *Identity* 2 (1982): 4–9.

18 Ibid., p. 6.

19 Ibid., p. 8.

20 Seamus Heaney, 'Speranza in Reading Gaol', in *The Redress of Poetry* (London: Faber & Faber, 1995), p. 95.

21 Lucy McDiarmid, 'Oscar Wilde's Speech from the Dock', in *The Wilde Legacy*, ed. Eileán Ní Chuilleanáin (Dublin: Four Courts, 2003). See this reference for an excellent and convincing argument against the idea of Wilde as an Irish patriot in the Old Bailey.

22 Linda Dowling, *Hellenism and Homosexuality in Victorian Oxford* (Ithaca, NY: Cornell University Press, 1994), p. 2.
23 Oscar Wilde, *The Collected Letters*, eds. Rupert Hart-Davis and Merlin Holland (London: Fourth Estate, 2000), p. 1019.
24 Ed Cohen, *Talk on the Wilde Side* (London: Routledge, 1993); Michael Foldy, *The Trials of Oscar Wilde: Deviance, Morality and Late-Victorian Society* (New Haven, Connecticut: Yale University Press, 1997).
25 Cohen, p. 181.
26 Declan Kiberd, *Inventing Ireland* (London: Jonathan Cape, 1995), pp. 35–36.
27 Oscar Wilde, *The Soul of Man under Socialism* (Oxford: Oxford University Press, 1990), p. 23.
28 Foldy, p. 70.
29 Ibid., p. 150.
30 Noreen Doody, 'An Influential Involvement: Wilde, Yeats and the French Symbolists', in *Critical Ireland*, eds. Aaron Kelly and Alan A. Gillis (Dublin: Four Courts, 2001), pp. 48–55.
31 H. Montgomery Hyde, *The Trials of Oscar Wilde* (Mineola, NY: Dover, 1974), p. 255.
32 Noreen Doody, 'Oscar Wilde: Nation and Empire', in *Palgrave Advances in Oscar Wilde Studies*, ed. Frederick Roden (London: Palgrave, 2004), p. 257.
33 *Galway Vindicator*, 5 June 1895.
34 *Cork Constitution*, 27 May 1895.
35 Cohen, *Talk on the Wilde Side*, p. 190.
36 *Freeman's Journal*, 27 May 1895.
37 Cohen, *Talk on the Wilde Side*, p. 185.
38 *Freeman's Journal*, 27 May 1895.
39 Ibid.
40 Ibid.
41 Hyde, *The Other Love*, p. 155.
42 Ibid.
43 Myles Dungan, *The Stealing of the Irish Crown Jewels* (Dublin: Townhouse, 2003), p. 93.
44 Ibid., p. 125.
45 *Gaelic American*, 4 July 1908. Quoted in Dungan, p. 182.
46 Sinfield, *The Wilde Century*, p. 125.

2. Nationalising Wilde: 1900–1928

1 Alan Sinfield, '"I See It Is My *Name* that Terrifies"', p. 142.
2 Lucy McDiarmid, *The Irish Art of Controversy*.
3 R.F. Foster, *Modern Ireland 1600–1972* (London: Penguin, 1988), p. 433.
4 Alan Sinfield, *The Wilde Century*, p. 124.
5 Margot Norris, 'A Walk on the Wild(e) Side', pp. 19–33.
6 McDiarmid, 'Oscar Wilde's Speech from the Dock', p. 115.
7 Ibid., p. 116.
8 Ibid., p. 117.
9 I am grateful to Margot Backus for this point.
10 McDiarmid, 'Oscar Wilde's Speech from the Dock', p. 126.
11 Ibid.
12 Ibid., p. 119.

13 Ibid., p. 133.

14 Margot, Backus, "'Odd Jobs": James Joyce, Oscar Wilde, and the Scandal Fragment', *Joyce Studies Annual*, 2008, p. 113.

15 Ibid., p. 117.

16 Ibid., p. 24.

17 I am grateful to Margot Backus for these comments, for all her insightful help into this chapter and for sharing her work on Joyce and scandal.

18 Daniel Corkery, *The Hidden Ireland* (Dublin: Gill & Macmillan, 1941).

19 Diarmaid Ferriter, *Occasions of Sin* (London: Profile Books, 2009), p. 68.

20 I am very thankful to David Rose of Oscholars for information on Wilde productions in Ireland.

21 L.C.P. Fox, 'People I Have Met', *Donohue's* (1905): 7.

22 *The Irish Times*, 21 December 1906.

23 *The Irish Times*, 27 December 1907, p. 7.

24 C.J. Hamilton, *Notable Irishwomen* (Dublin: Sealy, Bryers & Walker, 1905), p. 188.

25 *The Irish Times*, 21 September 1911, p. 7.

26 *The Irish Times*, 5 September 1913, p. 7.

27 *The Irish Times*, 13 February 1915, p. 7.

28 Elaine Sisson, *Pearse's Patriots* (Cork: Cork University Press, 2004), p. 140.

29 Susan C. Harris, *Gender and Modern Irish Drama* (Bloomington: Indiana University Press, 2002).

30 Ibid., p. 144.

31 Ibid., p. 160.

32 Jeffrey Dudgeon, *Roger Casement: The Black Diaries* (Belfast: Belfast Press, 2002), p. 16.

33 Harris, p. 145.

34 Lucy McDiarmid, *The Irish Art of Controversy*, p. 171.

35 See James Joyce, 'Oscar Wilde: The Poet of Salomé', in *The Critical Writings of James Joyce*, eds. John Mason and Richard Ellmann (London: Faber, 1959), p. 202.

36 Joyce, 'Oscar Wilde: The Poet of Salome', p. 204.

37 Ibid.

38 Ibid.

39 Joseph Valente (ed.), *Quare Joyce* (Ann Arbor: University of Michigan Press, 1998), p. 11.

40 See W.B. Yeats, *Autobiographies* (London: Macmillan, 1955), p. 285.

41 Yeats, *Autobiographies*, p. 287.

42 Yeats, *Autobiographies*, p. 291.

43 See Noreen Doody, 'An Influential Involvement: Wilde, Yeats and the French Symbolists', pp. 48–55.

44 H. Montgomery Hyde, *Oscar Wilde* (New York: Farrar, Straus and Giroux, 1975), p. 264.

45 Éibhear Walshe, 'Wilde's Irish Biographers', *The Wildean* 21 (July 2002): 15–27.

46 Joseph Bristow, *Effeminate England* (New York: Columbia University Press, 1995), p. 26.

47 Stanley Weintraub (ed.), *The Playwright and the Pirate* (Gerrards Cross: Colin Smythe, 1982), p. 33. See also Stanley Weintraub's essay on Wilde and Shaw in *Shaw's People: Victoria to Churchill* (Pennsylvania, PA: Pennsylvania State University Press, 1996).

48 Weintraub, *The Playwright and the Pirate*, p. 33.

49   Ibid., p. 37.
50   Quoted in Hyde, *Oscar Wilde*, p. 439.
51   Seamus Deane, *A Short History of Irish Literature* (Hutchinson: London, 1986), p. 135.
52   See Augusta Gregory, *The Journals*, vol. 2 (21 February 1925–29 May 1932), ed. Daniel. J. Murphy (Gerrards Cross: Colin Smythe, 1987), p. 241, 327.
53   Ibid., p. 366.
54   Ibid., p. 535.
55   Quoted in Tim Pat Coogan, *Michael Collins* (London: Hutchinson, 1990), p. 47.
56   Peter Hart, *Mick* (London: Macmillan, 2005), p. 342.
57   D.L. Kay, *The Glamour of Dublin* (Dublin: The Talbot Press, 1918), p. 73.
58   Sean O'Casey, The *Freeman's Journal*, 15 March 1924, p. 5.
59   *Connacht Tribune*, 4 December 1926, p. 3.
60   *The Irish Times*, 22 July 1954, p. 5.
61   Alla Nazimova was born Adelaide Leventon in Yalta, 4 June 1879. She moved to the USA in 1905 and died on 13 July 1945 in Los Angeles.
62   *The Irish Times*, 22 July 1954, p. 5.

3. WILDE IN THE NEW IRISH STATE: 1930–1960

1   Terence Brown, *Ireland: A Social and Cultural History 1922–2002* (London: Harper Perennial, 2004), p. 7.
2   Ibid., p. 7.
3   Maria Luddy, *Prostitution and Irish Society*, p. 157.
4   R.F. Foster, *Modern Ireland*, p. 516.
5   Brown, *Ireland*, pp. 142–43.
6   Tom Ingles, 'Origins and Legacies of Irish Prudery: Sexuality and Social Control in Modern Ireland', *Eire Ireland* 40, no. 3/4 (Fall/Winter, 2005): 21.
7   Cheryl Herr, 'The Erotics of Irishness', *Critical Inquiry* 17, no. 1 (Autumn, 1990): 1–34.
8   Diarmaid Ferriter, *The Transformation of Ireland 1900–2000* (London: Profile Books, 2004), p. 360.
9   Kieran Rose, *Diverse Communities: The Evolution of Lesbian and Gay Politics in Ireland* (Cork: Cork University Press, 1994), p. 8.
10   Diarmaid Ferriter, *Occasions of Sin*, p. 61.
11   *The Irish Times*, 13 February 1930, p. 6.
12   Owen Dudley Edwards, 'Oscar Wilde: The Soul of Man under Hibernicism', *Irish Studies Review* 3, no. 11 (1995): 11.
13   Edith Somerville, unpublished letter, 14 December 1935, William Andrews Clark Library, UCLA.
14   Somerville, unpublished letter, 4 January 1936.
15   Gifford Lewis, *The Selected Letters of Somerville and Ross* (London: Faber, 1989), pp. 67–68.
16   Ibid., p. 222.
17   Corkery, *The Hidden Ireland*, pp. xvi, xvii.
18   *The Irish Times*, 5 November 1937, p. 15.
19   Constantia Maxwell, *A History of Trinity College, 1591–1892* (Dublin: The University Press, 1946).
20   K.C. Bailey, *A History of Trinity College 1892–1945* (Dublin: The University Press, 1947), p. 197.
21   T.G. Wilson, 'Oscar Wilde at Trinity', *The Practitioner* 173 (October 1954): 473–80.

22 Ibid., pp. 473–74.

23 Ibid., p. 480.

24 R.B. McDowell and D.A. Webb, *Trinity College, Dublin: An Academic History* (Cambridge: Cambridge University Press, 1982).

25 J.V. Luce, *Trinity College Dublin: The First 400 Years* (Dublin: Trinity College Press, 1992), p. 9.

26 David Norris, 'The Green Carnation and the Queer Nation – Oscar Wilde Reclaimed', a lecture in memory of Oscar Wilde, commissioned by the post-graduate common room, Trinity College Dublin, October 1992, p. 16.

27 Lecture by Ian Stuart, Headmaster, Portora Royal School, for BBC Northern Ireland, 28 October 1937, published in the *Portora Royal School Register*. National Library of Ireland, Ir 379, p. 2.

28 Quoted in Deirdre Bair, *Samuel Beckett: A Biography* (London: Vintage, 1990), p. 35.

29 Norris, 'The Green Carnation', p. 14.

30 F.P. Carey, 'Historical Houses in the Irish Capital', *Irish Travel* 4, no. 1 (September, 1928): 10–11.

31 *The Irish Times*, 26 July 1941, p. 5.

32 *The Irish Times*, 30 May 1946, p. 7.

33 Kate O'Brien, *Farewell Spain* (London: Heinneman, 1937), p. 146.

34 Austin Clarke, *The Bell*, 1941, pp. 93–94.

35 Ibid., p. 94.

36 *Irish Independent*, 11 March 1941, p. 7.

37 Sean O'Faolain, *The Bell*, 2, 3 June 1941, p. 7.

38 Seanad Debate, November 1942, vol. 27, cols. 16–55, pp. 24–25.

39 See the bibliography in my biography, *Kate O'Brien: A Writing Life* (London: Irish Academic Press, 2006).

40 See my essay 'Wild(e) Irish', in *Ireland in Proximity*, ed. Alderson (London: Routledge, 1999), pp. 64–79.

41 T.G. Wilson, *Victorian Doctor* (London: Methuen, 1942), p. 1.

42 Ibid., p. 200.

43 Ibid., p. 303.

44 Ibid., p. 289.

45 Ibid., p. 324.

46 I am very grateful to Jeff Dudgeon for his generosity in sharing his research on Hyde and allowing me to draw from his essay 'The Struggle for Political Survival of Hartford Montgomery Hyde', presented at the Wolfenden 50 conference in June 2007 at the University of London.

47 *Oscar Wilde* (1975); *Oscar Wilde: The Aftermath* (1963); *Lord Alfred Douglas* (1984).

48 H. Montgomery Hyde, *The Trials of Oscar Wilde* (London: William Hodge & Company, 1948).

49 H. Montgomery Hyde, *The Other Love: An Historical and Contemporary Survey of Homosexuality in Britain* (London: Heinemann, 1970), pp. 210–11.

50 Hansard, Commons Debates, vol. 552, cols. 749–60.

51 'A Man for All Seasons', *The Irish Times*, 5 January 1985, p. 11.

52 These and many other relevant cuttings are in the Lesbian and Gay Newsmedia Archive (LAGNA) at Middlesex University, http://www.lagna.org.uk/archive/cuttings.

53 *The Irish Times*, 6 August 1949, p. 4.

54 Ibid.
55 Brown, *Ireland*, pp. 214–15.
56 Tom Garvin, *Preventing the Future: Why Ireland Was So Poor for so Long* (Dublin: Gill & Macmillan, 2004), p. 4.
57 Matt Cook, *A Gay History of Britain* (Oxford: Greenwood World Publishing, 2007), p. 186.
58 Patrick Ryan, *The Wildes of Merrion Square* (London: Staples Press, 1953), p. 57.
59 Ibid., p. 120.
60 Ibid., p. 191.
61 Ibid., p. 192.
62 Ibid., p. 194.
63 Ibid., pp. 201–02.
64 Ibid., p. 203.
65 *The Irish Times*, 3 April 1953, p. 6.
66 St John Ervine, *Oscar Wilde*, p. 7.
67 Ibid., p. 7.
68 Ibid., p. 9.
69 Ibid., p. 12.
70 Ibid., p. 16.
71 Ibid., pp. 36–39.
72 Ibid., p. 41.
73 Ibid., p. 246.
74 Ibid., p. 52.
75 Ibid., p. 244.
76 Ibid., p. 81.
77 Ibid., pp. 64–65.
78 Ibid., p. 80.
79 Ibid., p. 176.
80 Ibid., pp. 328–29.
81 Ibid., p. 336.
82 *The Irish Times*, 22 July 1954, p. 5.
83 Myles na Gopaleen, *The Irish Times*, 11 September 1954, p. 4.
84 *The Irish Times*, 14 September 1954, p. 8.
85 Christopher Fitz-Simon, *The Boys* (Dublin: Gill and Macmillan, 2004), p. 217.
86 *Evening Herald*, 16 October 1954, p. 1.
87 Micheál mac Líammóir, *The Irish Times*, 19 October 1954, p. 9.
88 Lennox Robinson, 'Oscar Wilde', in *I Sometimes Think* (Dublin: Talbot Press, 1956), p. 105.
89 Ibid., pp. 105–06.
90 Ibid., p. 108.
91 *Sunday Independent*, 17 October 1954, p. 9.
92 *The Irish Times*, 21 October 1954, p. 11.
93 *Evening Herald*, 14 October 1954, p. 5.
94 *Evening Herald*, 27 October 1954.
95 *Ireland of the Welcomes* 4, no. 3 (September–October, 1955): 21–3.
96 Michael O'Sullivan, *Brendan Behan's Life* (Dublin: Blackwater, 1997), p. 63.
97 Ibid., p. 139.
98 Ibid., p. 181.
99 Ibid., pp. 150–51.

100 Patrick Kavanagh, *Irish Farmers' Journal*, 8 October 1960, p. 22.

101 Shane Leslie, 'Oscar Wilde and Catholicism', *The Month* 28, no. 5 (October, 1962): 234.

102 Ibid., p. 236.

103 I am grateful to Tomás Irish for researching the travel books and guides to Dublin included in this chapter. For example: Philip Rooney, 'Irish Holiday', *Ireland of the Welcomes* 6, no. 5 (January–February 1958): 4–7 (a very general article on things to do in Ireland); 'Dublin Offers Its Visitors a Diversity of Literary Pilgrimages', *Ireland of the Welcomes* 6, no. 5, 6 (references Shaw, Joyce, Yeats and O'Casey, but not Wilde); 'An Tóstal', *Ireland of the Welcomes* 8, no. 3 (September–October 1959): 8–9 (an article about An Tóstal, Ireland's springtime festival; references 'Dublin's great theatrical tradition' and names Goldsmith, Sheridan, Shaw and O'Casey, but not Wilde).

104 *Ireland of the Welcomes* 8, no. 3 (September–October 1959): 14–17.

105 *Ireland of the Welcomes* 10, no. 1 (May–June 1961): p. 35.

106 David Cairns and Shaun Richards, *Writing Ireland: Colonialism, Nationalism and Culture* (Manchester: Manchester University Press, 1988), p. 139.

4. The mac Líammóir revolution: 1960–1970

1 Micheál mac Líammóir, *An Oscar of no Importance* (London: Heinemann, 1968), p. 25, hereafter ONI.

2 Ibid., p. 131.

3 From *Did You Know that the Gate*, Gate Theatre programme, 1940, p. 1.

4 Terence Brown, *Ireland: A Social and Cultural History 1922–2002*, new edn (London: Harper Perennial, 2004), p. 137.

5 Christopher Fitz-Simon, *The Boys*, p. 41.

6 Alan Sinfield, *The Wilde Century*, p. 11.

7 Micheál mac Líammóir, *All for Hecuba* (London: Methuen, 1946), p. 25, hereafter AFH.

8 Ibid., p. 30.

9 Micheál mac Líammóir, *Theatre in Ireland* (Dublin: Colm Ó Lochlainn, 1950), p. 25.

10 AFH, p. 229.

11 Ibid., p. 45.

12 Ibid., p. 32.

13 Ibid., p. 215.

14 Ibid., p. 70.

15 Ibid., p. 331.

16 Brown, p. 167.

17 Mac Líammóir, *Theatre in Ireland*, p. 222.

18 Hilton Edwards to Micheál mac Líammóir, 30 August 1957, Gate Theatre archive, North-Western University, Chicago. I am grateful to Joan Dean for allowing me to read her essay 'mac Líammóir's Oscar and the American Reclamation of Wilde'.

19 E.M. Forster, *Maurice* (Harmondsworth: Penguin, 1972), p. 136.

20 H. Montgomery Hyde, *The Other Love*, p. 233.

21 Fitz-Simon, *The Boys*, p. 231.

22 *Irish Press*, 20 September 1960, p. 4.

23 *The Irish Times*, 20 September 1960, p. 5.

24 *Irish Independent*, 20 September 1960, p. 2.

25 Micheál Ó hAodha, *The Importance of Being Micheál: A Portrait of mac Líammóir* (Dingle, County Kerry: Brandon Book Publishing, 1990), p. 159.
26 Hilton Edwards, Introduction to *The Importance of Being Oscar*, by Micheál mac Líammóir, p. 5.
27 Micheál mac Líammóir, *The Importance of Being Oscar* (Dublin: Dolmen Press, 1963), p. 15, hereafter IBO.
28 Ibid., p. 37.
29 *New Yorker*, 25 March 1961.
30 *World Telegraph and Sun*, 15 March 1961.
31 See Joan Fitzpatrick Dean, 'mac Líammóir's *The Importance of Being Oscar* in America', in *Irish Theater in America*, ed., John P. Harrington (Syracuse University Press, 2009).
32 Mac Líammóir, ONI, p. 138.
33 Alan Sinfield, *Out On Stage* (New Haven, Connecticut: Yale University Press, 1999), p. 265.
34 ONI, p. 1.
35 Ibid., p. 4.
36 Ibid., p. 24.
37 Ibid., p. 29.
38 Ibid., p. 62.
39 Ibid., p. 63.
40 Ibid., p. 131.
41 Ibid., p. 223.
42 Ibid., p. 47.
43 Fitz-Simon, *The Boys*, p. 295.
44 Ibid.
45 Micheál mac Líammóir, '*Prelude in Kasbek Street*', in *Selected Plays of Micheál mac Líammóir* (Gerrards Cross: Colin Smythe, 1998), hereafter PKS. Written in 1973.
46 Ibid., p. 14.
47 Ibid., p. 257.
48 Ibid., p. 261.
49 Ibid., p. 262.
50 Fitz-Simon, *The Boys*, p. 299.
51 Ibid.

5. Reinventing Wilde the Irishman: 1960–2000

1 Dermot Keogh, *Twentieth-Century Ireland: Nation and State* (Dublin: Gill & Macmillan, 1994), p. 243.
2 Diarmaid Ferriter, *Occasions of Sin*, p. 391.
3 J.J. Lee, *Ireland: Politics and Society 1912–1985* (Cambridge: Cambridge University Press, 1989), p. 645.
4 Tom Garvin, *Preventing the Future*, p. 209.
5 Diarmaid Ferriter, *The Transformation of Ireland*, p. 117.
6 David Norris, *The Irish Times*, 25 June 1993, p. 12.
7 Fintan O'Toole, 'Irish Literature in English in the New Millennium', in *The Cambridge History of Irish Literature*, Volume II, 1890–2000, eds. Margaret Kelleher and Philip O'Leary (Cambridge: Cambridge University Press, 2006), p. 641.
8 H. Montgomery Hyde, *Oscar Wilde: The Aftermath* (New York: Farrar, Straus & Giroux, 1963), p. xxi.

9   Ibid., p. 2.

10 Ibid., p. 7.

11 Ibid., p. 94.

12 Terence de Vere White, *The Parents of Oscar Wilde* (London: Hodder & Stoughton, 1967), p. 17.

13 Ibid., p. 17.

14 Ibid.

15 Ibid., p. 19.

16 Ibid., p. 155.

17 Ibid., pp. 267–69.

18 Terence de Vere White, *The Anglo-Irish* (London: Victor Gollancz, 1972), p. 197.

19 Ibid., p. 200.

20 H. Montgomery Hyde, *The Other Love*, p. 2.

21 Ibid., p. 269.

22 Ibid., p. 304.

23 H. Montgomery Hyde, *Oscar Wilde*.

24 Ibid., p. 204.

25 Ibid., p. 205.

26 Ibid., p. 210.

27 Ibid., p. 439.

28 *Sunday Independent*, 20 June 1976, p. 9.

29 *The Pilgrimage* (London: Weidenfeld & Nicolson, 1961); *The Fugitives* (London: Weidenfeld & Nicolson, 1962); *Don Juaneen* (London: Weidenfeld & Nicolson, 1963); *The Waking of Willie Ryan* (London: Weidenfeld & Nicolson, 1965); *An Apology for Roses* (London: Calder & Boyars, 1973); *The Flood* (London: Marion Boyars, 1987); and *The Irish Magdalen* (London: Marion Boyars, 1991).

30 John Broderick, 'The Apotheosis of Wilde', *Irish Independent*, 24 May 1976.

31 Julia Carlson, 'John Broderick Interview', in *Banned in Ireland: Censorship and the Irish Writer* (London: Routledge, 1990), p. 46.

32 John Jordan (1930–1988) was a poet, critic and short-story writer. His publications include *A Raft from Flotsam: Versifications 1948–1974* (Oldcastle: Gallery Press, 1975); *Blood and Stations* (poems and prose) (Gallery Press, 1976); *Yarns* (stories) (Dublin: Poolbeg, 1977); and a posthumous *Collected Poems* (Dublin: The Dedalus Press, 1990). Lilliput Press published a selection of his prose in 2006.

33 John Jordan, 'Rupert Hart-Davis's *The Letters of Oscar Wilde*', *Hibernia* (26 July 1979). This review can be found in Hugh McFadden, ed., *Crystal Clear: The Selected Prose of John Jordan* (Dublin: Lilliput Books, 2006), p. 77.

34 My thanks to Tonie Walsh, curator of the Irish Queer Archive, for help in locating these articles. The Irish Queer Archive is now located in the National Library of Ireland and contains the entire run of *Identity* magazine, as well as all Irish lesbian and gay periodicals.

35 All these articles can be found in *Identity*, a gay magazine published in Dublin by the National Gay Federation in the early 1980s.

36 Richard Pine, *Oscar Wilde* (Dublin: Gill & Macmillan, 1983), p. vii.

37 Owen Dudley Edwards, *The Fireworks of Oscar Wilde* (London: Barrie & Jenkins, 1989).

38 Ibid., pp. 21–22.

39 Ibid., p. 29.

40 David Norris, 'The Green Carnation and the Queer Nation – Oscar Wilde Reclaimed', a lecture in memory of Oscar Wilde commissioned by the post-graduate common room, Trinity College Dublin, October 1992. I am grateful to Senator Norris for this copy of his unpublished lecture.

41 Ibid., p. 1.

42 Ibid., pp. 3–4.

43 Ibid., pp. 44–45.

44 Davis Coakley, *Oscar Wilde: The Importance of Being Irish* (Dublin: Townhouse, 1994).

45 Neil McKenna, *The Secret Life of Oscar Wilde* (London: Century, 2003).

46 Coakley, p. 2.

47 Ibid., p. 4.

48 Ibid., p. 195.

49 Ibid., p. 206.

50 Ibid.

51 Vivian Mercier, *The Irish Comic Tradition* (Oxford: Oxford University Press, 1962), pp. xii.

52 Seamus Deane, *A Short History of Irish Literature*, p. 134.

53 Neil Sammells, 'Rediscovering the Wilde Irish', in *Rediscovering Oscar Wilde*, ed. C. George Sandulescu (Gerrards Cross: Colin Smythe, 1994), pp. 362–63.

54 Ibid., p. 363.

55 Seamus Deane, general editor, *The Field Day Anthology of Irish Writing*, 3 vols. (Derry: Field Day, 1991).

56 Sammells, p. 365.

57 Ibid., p. 369.

58 Declan Kiberd, Introduction to 'The London Exiles: Wilde and Shaw' in *The Field Day Anthology of Irish Writing*, vol. 2, ed. Deane (Derry: Field Day, 1991), p. 372.

59 Declan Kiberd, *Inventing Ireland*, p. 34.

60 Ibid., p. 36.

61 Ibid., p. 39.

62 Ibid., p. 44.

63 Declan Kiberd, *Irish Classics* (London: Granta, 2000).

64 Ibid., p. 325.

65 Ibid., p. 327.

66 Ibid., p. 334.

67 Ibid., p. 335.

68 Richard Pine, *The Thief of Reason*, p. 16.

69 Ibid., p. 17.

70 Ibid., p. 23.

71 Ibid., p. 36.

72 Ibid., p. 129.

73 Ibid., p. 156.

74 Ibid., p. 348.

75 Ibid., p. 383.

76 McCormack, *Wilde the Irishman*, p. 1.

77 Ibid., p. 2.

78 Ibid.

79 Ibid.

80 Ibid., p. 3.

81 Ibid., p. 5.

82 Deirdre Toomey, 'Wilde and Orality', in *Wilde the Irishman*, ed. Jerusha McCormack, p. 34.

83 Bernard O'Donoghue, 'The Journey to Reading Gaol: Sacrifice and Scapegoats in Irish Literature', in *Wilde the Irishman*, ed. Jerusha McCormack, p. 104.

84 Ibid., p. 108.

85 Derek Mahon, 'Ellmann's Wilde', in *Wilde the Irishman*, ed. Jerusha McCormack, p. 147.

86 Ibid.

87 Ibid., p. 150.

88 *The Irish Times*, 29 October 1997, p. 14.

89 Ibid.

90 *The Irish Times*, 8 December 1997.

91 Noreen Doody, 'Performance and Place: Oscar Wilde and the Irish National Interest', in *The Reception of Oscar Wilde in Europe*, ed. Stefano Evangelista (London: Continuum, 2010), p. 63.

92 http://www.tcd.ie/OWC/

93 *The Irish Times*, 23 June 2000, p. 14.

6. IMAGINING WILDE THE IRISHMAN: 1980–2000

1 R.F. Foster, *Luck and the Irish* (London: Allen Lane, 2007), p. 181.

2 Fintan O'Toole, p. 629.

3 Linden Peach, *The Contemporary Irish Novel* (London: Palgrave, 2004), p. 7.

4 Ibid., p. 9.

5 Gerry Smyth, 'Decolonisation and Criticism: Towards a Theory of Irish Critical Discourse', in *Ireland and Cultural Theory: The Mechanics of Authenticity*, ed. Colin Graham and Richard Kirkland (Basingstoke: Palgrave Macmillan, 1999), p. 38.

6 Ibid., p. 38.

7 Noreen Doody, p. 90.

8 Glyn Davis, 'Taming Oscar Wilde', in *British Queer Cinema*, ed. Robin Griffiths (London: Routledge, 2006), pp. 199–201.

9 Declan Kiberd, *The Irish Writer and the World* (Cambridge: Cambridge University Press, 2005), p. 256.

10 Edna O'Brien, 'Dramas', *The Paris Review* 110 (1989): 176.

11 Ibid., p. 180.

12 Seamus Heaney, 'Speranza in Reading Gaol', p. 95.

13 Seamus Heaney, RTÉ Radio 1992. Quoted in Davis Coakley, *Oscar Wilde: The Importance of Being Irish*, p. 212.

14 Seamus Heaney, 'Oscar Wilde Dedication: Westminster Abbey, 14 February 1995', in Jerusha McCormack, pp. 174–75.

15 Peter Dickinson, 'Oscar Wilde: Reading the Life After the Life' *Biography* 28, no. 3, Summer 2005, 416.

16 Lucia Kramer, 'Of Doormats and Iced Champagne: The Wilde Trials in Fictional Biography' in *The Importance of Reinventing Oscar*, eds. Uwe Boker, Richard Corballis and Julie A. Hibbard (Rodopi, Amsterdam: 2002), p. 202.

17 *The Irish Times*, 1 November 1989, p. 12. The Guildford pub bombings occurred on 5 October 1974, when the IRA planted two bombs in pubs in Guildford. The Guildford Four were Gerry Conlon, Paul Hill, Patrick Armstrong and Carole Richardson. The bombings were at the height of the Troubles in Northern

Ireland and in Decemaber 1974 the plice arrested these four, later to be known as the Guildford Four. They were released fifteen years later and their convictions overturned.

18 Terry Eagleton, *St Oscar* (Derry: Field Day, 1989), p. xi.
19 Ibid., p. viii.
20 Ibid., pp. x–xi.
21 Ibid., p. viii.
22 Ibid., p. 6.
23 Dickinson, p .418.
24 Ibid., p. 6.
25 Ibid., pp. 13–17.
26 Ibid., p. 19.
27 *The Irish Times*, 10 October 1997, p. 1.
28 Frank McGuinness, 'An Interview with Jacqueline Hurtley', in *Ireland in Writing: Interviews with Writers and Academics*, eds. Jacqueline Hurtley et al. (Amsterdam and Atlanta, Georgia: Ropopi, 1998), p. 254.
29 Frank McGuinness, 'The Spirit of Play in Oscar Wilde's *De Profundis*', in *Creativity and Its Contexts*, ed. Chris Morash (Dublin: Lilliput, 1995), p. 52.
30 *The Irish Times*, 2 October 1997, p. 12.
31 Thomas Kilroy, *The Secret Fall of Constance Wilde* (Dublin: Gallery Press, 1997), p. 66.
32 Ibid., p. 20.
33 Ibid., p. 30.
34 Ibid., p. 68.
35 *The Irish Times*, 9 October 1997, pp. 13–14.
36 *The Irish Times*, 15 October 1997, p. 15.
37 *The Irish Times*, 21 October 1997, p. 15.
38 Maria Pramaggiore, '"Papa Don't Preach": Pregnancy and Performance in Contemporary Irish Cinema', in *The Irish in US: Irishness, Performativity, and Popular Culture*, ed. Diane Negra (Durham, NC: Duke University Press, 2006), p. 125.
39 Ibid., pp. 124–25.
40 *Irish Independent*, 21 April 1995, p. 26.
41 *The Irish Times*, 21 April 1995, p. 15.
42 Kathryn Conrad, *Occupied Country:The Negotiation of Lesbianism in Irish Feminist Narrative, Eire/Ireland* (Spring 1996), 135.
43 Emma Donoghue, 'Noises from Woodsheds: Tales of Irish Lesbians 1886–1989', in *Towards The Twenty-First Century*, ed. Eoin Collins (Cassells: London, 1995). p. 159. Also see my essay 'The Fictions of Emma Donoghue', in *The UCD Aesthetic*, ed. Anthony Roche (Dublin: New Island Books, 2005), p. 274.
44 Colm Tóibín, *Love in a Dark Time: Gay Lives from Wilde to Almodovar* (London: Picador, 2003), p 1.
45 See my essay '"This Particular Genie": The Elusive Gay Male Body in Tóibín's Novels' in *Reading Colm Tóibín*, Paul Delaney, ed. (Dublin: The Liffey Press, 2008), pp. 115–31 for a fuller discussion of Tóibín's representation of contemporary Irish gay identity.

7. WILDE IN THE TWENTY-FIRST CENTURY: 2000–2010
  1 *The Irish Times*, 1 December 2000, p. 9.

2   News release by the Northern Ireland Department of Culture, Arts and Leisure, 13 June 2003.

3   Heather White, *Wilde Fire* (Enniskillen, Fermanagh: Principia Press, 2002); Heather White, *A Wilde Family* (Fermanagh: Principia Press, 2002).

4   Eiléan Ní Chuilleanáin, ed., *The Wilde Legacy* (Dublin: Four Courts Press, 2003).

5   Ibid., p. 9.

6   Ibid., p. 11.

7   Ibid., p. 13.

8   Lucy McDiarmid, 'Oscar Wilde's Speech from the Dock', in Ní Chuilleanáin, *The Wilde Legacy*, p. 115.

9   Ibid., p. 116.

10   Ibid., p. 117.

11   Ibid., p. 133.

12   Alan Sinfield, '"I See It Is My *Name* that Terrifies"', p. 137.

13   Ibid., p. 142.

14   Ibid., p. 143.

15   Ibid., p. 145.

16   Ibid.

17   Ibid., p. 146.

18   Ibid., p. 150.

19   Ibid., pp. 150–51.

20   Ibid., p. 151.

21   Jarlath Killeen, *The Faiths of Oscar Wilde* (Hampshire: Palgrave, 2005), p. 1.

22   Ibid., p. 9.

23   Ibid., p. 65.

24   Ibid., p. 77.

25   Ibid., p. 89.

26   Ibid., p. 108.

27   Jarlath Killeen, *The Fairy Tales of Oscar Wilde* (Aldershot: Ashgate, 2007), p. 1.

28   Ibid., p. 17.

29   Ibid., p. 171.

30   Thomas Kilroy, *My Scandalous Life* (Oldcastle: The Gallery Press, 2004), p. 9.

31   Ibid., pp. 25–26.

32   Ibid., p. 26.

33   Gregory Woods, *A History of Gay Literature* (New Haven and London: Yale University Press, 1998), p. 9.

34   Dermod Moore, *Diary of a Man* (Dublin: Hot Press Books, 2005), p. 190.

35   Matthew Sturgis, *Passionate Attitudes: The English Decadence of the Eighteen Nineties* (London: Macmillan, 1995), p. 299.

36   Ibid.

37   Anne Mulhall, 'Camping Up the Emerald Isle: "Queerness" in Irish Popular Culture', in *Irish Postmodernisms and Popular Culture*, eds. Mulhall Balzano, and Sullivan (Basingstoke: Palgrave Macmillan, 2007), p. 65.

38   Annamarie Jagose, *Queer Theory* (Melbourne: Melbourne University Press, 1996), p. 3.

39   Fintan Walsh, *Queer Notions: New Plays and Performances from Ireland* (Cork: Cork University Press, 2010), p. 4.

40   Matt Cook, 'Wilde Lives: Derek Jarman and the Queer Eighties', in *Oscar Wilde and Modern Culture*, ed. Joseph Bristow (Athens, Ohio: Ohio University Press, 2008), p. 286.

41   Jamie O'Neill, *At Swim, Two Boys* (London: Scribner, 2001), p. 436.
42   Ibid., pp. 436–37.
43   Ibid., p. 438.
44   Ibid., p. 309.
45   David Halperin, 'Pal o' Me Heart', *London Review of Books* 25, no. 10 (22 May 2003), 32–33.
46   Colm Tóibín, *Love in a Dark Time*, p. 7.
47   Ibid., p. 14.
48   Ibid., p. 46.
49   Ibid., p. 51.
50   Ibid., p. 60.
51   Ibid., p. 61.
52   Ibid., p. 86.
53   Colm Tóibín, *The Master* (London: Picador, 2004), p. 71.
54   Ibid., pp. 72–73.
55   Ibid., p. 100.
56   Ibid.
57   Ibid., pp. 310–11.
58   Colm Tóibín, *Love in a Dark Time*, p. 26.
59   *The Irish Times*, 27 July 2005, p. 12.
60   Ibid.
61   Brian Lacey, *Terrible Queer Creatures* (Dublin: Wordwell, 2008).
62   Ibid., p. 156.
63   *The Irish Times*, 14 May 2010.

Bibliography

Backus, Margot, "'Odd Jobs'": James Joyce, Oscar Wilde, and the Scandal Fragment' *Joyce Studies Annual*, 2008.

Bailey, K.C., *A History of Trinity College 1892–1945* (Dublin: The University Press, 1947), p. 197.

Boker, Uwe, ed., *The Importance of Reinventing Oscar* (Amsterdam: Rodopi, 2002).

Breen, T.C., 'Loathsome, Impure and Revolting Crimes: The Dublin Scandals of 1884', *Identity* 2 (1982): 4–9.

Bristow, Joseph, *Effeminate England* (New York: Columbia University Press, 1995).

—, Joseph, *Oscar Wilde and Modern Culture* (Ohio: Ohio University Press, 2008).

Brown, Terence, *Ireland: A Social and Cultural History 1922–2002* (London: Harper Perennial, 2004).

Cairns, David, and Shaun Richards, *Writing Ireland: Colonialism, Nationalism and Culture* (Manchester: Manchester University Press, 1988).

Carey, F.P., 'Historical Houses in the Irish Capital', *Irish Travel* 4, no. 1 (September, 1928): 10–11.

Carlson, Julia, 'John Broderick Interview', in *Banned in Ireland: Censorship and the Irish Writer* (London: Routledge, 1990).

Coakley, Davis, *Oscar Wilde: The Importance of Being Irish* (Dublin: Townhouse, 1994).

Cohen, Ed, *Talk on the Wilde Side* (London: Routledge, 1993).

Conrad, Kathryn, 'Occupied Country: The Negotiation of Lesbianism in Irish Feminist Narrative', *Eire/Ireland* 31, no. 1 & 2 (Spring/Summer 1996).

Coogan, Tim Pat, *Michael Collins* (London: Hutchinson, 1990).

Cook, Matt, *A Gay History of Britain* (Oxford: Greenwood World Publishing, 2007).

—, *London and the Culture of Homosexuality, 1885–1914* (Cambridge: Cambridge University Press, 2003).

Corkery, Daniel, *The Hidden Ireland* (Dublin: Gill & Macmillan, 1941).

Davis, Glyn, 'Taming Oscar Wilde', in *British Queer Cinema*, ed. Robin Griffiths (London: Routledge, 2006), pp. 199–201.

de Vere White, Terence, *The Anglo-Irish* (London: Victor Gollancz, 1972).

— (ed.), *The Parents of Oscar Wilde* (London: Hodder & Stoughton, 1967).

Dean, Joan Fitzpatrick, 'mac Líammóir's *The Importance of Being Oscar* in America'. in *Irish Theater in America*, ed., John P. Harrington (Syracuse University Press, 2009).

Deane, Seamus, *A Short History of Irish Literature* (Hutchinson: London, 1986).
— (ed.), *The Field Day Anthology of Irish Writing*, 3 vols. (Derry: Field Day, 1991).
Dickinson, Peter. 'Oscar Wilde: Reading the Life After the Life', *Biography* 28, no. 3 (Summer 2005).
Doody, Noreen, 'An Influential Involvement: Wilde, Yeats and the French Symbolists', in *Critical Ireland*, eds. Aaron Kelly and Alan A .Gillis (Dublin: Four Courts Press, 2001).
—, 'Oscar Wilde: Nation and Empire', in *Palgrave Advances in Oscar Wilde Studies*, ed. Frederick Roden (London: Palgrave, 2004).
—, 'Performance and Place: Oscar Wilde and the Irish National Interest', in *The Reception of Oscar Wilde in Europe*, ed. Stefano Evangelista (London: Continuum, 2010).
Dowling, Linda, *Hellenism and Homosexuality in Victorian Oxford* (Ithaca, NY: Cornell University Press, 1994).
Dudgeon, Jeffrey, *Roger Casement: The Black Diaries* (Belfast: Belfast Press, 2002).
Dudley, Anthony, *Oscar in the Wildes: The Wilde Family in Connemara and Mayo* (Dublin: Ashfield Press, 2003).
Dudley Edwards, Owen, 'Impressions of an Irish Sphinx', in *Wilde the Irishman*, ed. Jerusha McCormack (New Haven, Connecticut and London: Yale University Press, 1998).
—, 'Oscar Wilde: The Soul of Man under Hibernicism', *Irish Studies Review* 3, no. 11 (1995).
—, *The Fireworks of Oscar Wilde* (London: Barrie & Jenkins, 1989).
Dungan, Myles, *The Stealing of the Irish Crown Jewels* (Dublin: Townhouse, 2003).
Eagleton, Terry, *St Oscar* (Derry: Field Day, 1989).
Edwards, Hilton, Introduction to *The Importance of Being Oscar*, by Micheál mac Líammóir (Dublin: Dolmen Press, 1963), p. 5.
Ervine, St John, *Oscar Wilde: A Present Time Appraisal* (New York: Morrow, 1952).
Ferriter, Diarmaid, *The Occasions of Sin* (London: Profile Books, 2009).
—, *The Transformation of Ireland 1900–2000* (London: Profile Books, 2004).
Fitz-Simon, Christopher, *The Boys: A Biography of Micheál mac Líammóir and Hilton Edwards* (Dublin: Gill & Macmillan, 1994).
Foldy, Michael, *The Trials of Oscar Wilde: Deviance, Morality and Late-Victorian Society* (New Haven, Connecticut: Yale University Press, 1997).
Forster, E.M., *Maurice* (Harmondsworth: Penguin, 1972).
Foster, R.F., *Luck and the Irish* (London: Allen Lane, 2007).
—, R.F., *Modern Ireland 1600–1972* (London: Penguin, 1988).
Fox, L.C.P., 'People I Have Met', *Donohue's* (1905): 7.
Garvin, Tom, *Preventing the Future: Why Ireland Was so Poor for so Long* (Dublin: Gill & Macmillan, 2004).
Gregory, Augusta, *The Journals*, vol. 2 (21 February 1925 to 29 May 1932), ed. Daniel J. Murphy (Gerrards Cross: Colin Smythe, 1987), p. 241.

Halperin, David, 'Pal o' Me Heart', *London Review of Books* (22 May 2003).

Hamilton, C.J., *Notable Irishwomen* (Dublin: Sealy, Bryers and Walker, 1905).

Harris, Susan C., *Gender and Modern Irish Drama* (Bloomington: Indiana University Press, 2002).

Hart, Peter, *Mick* (London: Macmillan, 2005), p. 342.

Heaney, Seamus, 'Oscar Wilde Dedication: Westminster Abbey, 14 February 1995', in *Wilde the Irishman*, ed. Jerusha McCormack (New Haven Connecticut and London: Yale University Press, 1998), pp. 174–75.

—, 'Speranza in Reading Gaol', in *The Redress of Poetry* (London: Faber & Faber, 1995).

Herr, Cheryl, 'The Erotics of Irishness', *Critical Inquiry* 17, no. 1 (Autumn 1990): 1–34.

Hyde, H. Montgomery, *Oscar Wilde* (New York: Farrar, Straus & Giroux, 1975).

—, *Oscar Wilde: The Aftermath* (New York: Farrar, Straus & Giroux, 1963).

—, *The Other Love: An Historical and Contemporary Survey of Homosexuality in Britain* (London: Heinemann, 1970).

—, *The Trials of Oscar Wilde* (London: William Hodge & Company, 1948).

—, *The Trials of Oscar Wilde* (Mineola, NY: Dover, 1974).

Ingles, Tom, 'Origins and Legacies of Irish Prudery: Sexuality and Social Control in Modern Ireland', *Eire Ireland* 40, no. 3/4 (Fall/Winter 2005): 21.

Jagose, Annamarie, *Queer Theory* (Melbourne: Melbourne University Press, 1996.

Jordan, John, 'Rupert Hart-Davis's *The Letters of Oscar Wilde*', *Hibernia* (26 July 1979).

Joyce, James, 'Oscar Wilde: The Poet of Salomé', in *The Critical Writings of James Joyce*, ed. John Mason and Richard Ellmann (London: Faber, 1959).

Kavanagh, Patrick, *Irish Farmers' Journal* (8 October, 1960), p. 22.

Kay, D.L., *The Glamour of Dublin* (Dublin: The Talbot Press, 1918), p. 73.

Keogh, Dermot, *Twentieth-Century Ireland: Nation and State* (Dublin: Gill & Macmillan, 1994).

Kiberd, Declan, *Inventing Ireland* (London: Jonathan Cape, 1995).

—, *Irish Classics* (London: Granta, 2000)

—, 'The London Exiles: Wilde and Shaw', in *The Field Day Anthology of Irish Writing*, vol. 2, ed. Seamus Deane (Derry: Field Day, 1991), pp. 372–515.

—, *The Irish Writer and the World* (Cambridge: Cambridge University Press, 2005).

Killeen, Jarlath, *The Fairy Tales of Oscar Wilde* (Aldershot: Ashgate, 2007).

—, *The Faiths of Oscar Wilde* (Hampshire: Palgrave, 2005).

Kilroy, Thomas, *My Scandalous Life* (Oldcastle, County Meath: The Gallery Press, 2004).

—, *The Secret Fall of Constance Wilde* (Dublin: Gallery Press, 1997).

Lacey, Brian *Terrible Queer Creatures* (Dublin: Wordswell, 2008).

Lee, J.J., *Ireland: Politics and Society 1912–1985* (Cambridge: Cambridge University Press, 1989), p. 645.

Leslie, Shane, 'Oscar Wilde and Catholicism', *The Month* 28, no. 5 (October 1962): 234.

Lewis, Gifford, *The Selected Letters of Somerville and Ross* (London: Faber, 1989), pp. 67–68.

Luce, J.V., *Trinity College Dublin: The First 400 Years* (Dublin: Trinity College Press, 1992).

Luddy, Maria, *Prostitution and Irish Society, 1800–1940* (Cambridge: Cambridge University Press, 2008).

mac Líammóir, Micheál, 'Prelude in Kasbek Street', in *Selected Plays of Micheál mac Líammóir* (Gerrards Cross: Colin Smythe, 1998). Written in 1973.

—, *All for Hecuba* (London: Methuen, 1946).

—, *An Oscar of no Importance* (Dublin: Dolmen Press, 1963).

—, *The Importance of Being Oscar* (Dublin: Heinemann, 1963).

—, *Theatre in Ireland* (Dublin: Colm Ó Lochlainn, 1950).

—, *Enter a Goldfish: Memoirs of an Irish Actor, Young and Old* (London: Thames & Hudson, 1977).

Mahon, Derek, 'Ellmann's Wilde', in *Wilde the Irishman*, ed. Jerusha McCormack (New Haven, Connecticut and London: Yale University Press, 1998), p. 147.

Maxwell, Constantia, *A History of Trinity College, 1591–1892* (Dublin: The University Press, 1946).

McCormack, Jerusha, ed., *Wilde the Irishman* (New Haven, Connecticut and London: Yale University Press, 1998).

McDiarmid, Lucy, 'Oscar Wilde's Speech from the Dock', in *The Wilde Legacy*, ed. Eileán Ní Chuilleanáin (Dublin: Four Courts, 2003), pp. 113–35.

—, *The Irish Art of Controversy* (Dublin: Lilliput, 2005).

McDowell, R.B., and D.A. Webb, *Trinity College, Dublin: An Academic History* (Cambridge: Cambridge University Press, 1982).

McGuinness, Frank 'The Spirit of Play in Oscar Wilde's *De Profundis*', in *Creativity and Its Contexts*, ed. Chris Morash (Dublin: Lilliput, 1995).

—, 'An Interview with Jacqueline Hurtley', in *Ireland in Writing: Interviews with Writers and Academics*, eds. Jacqueline Hurtley et al. (Amsterdam and Atlanta, Georgia: Rodopi, 1998), p. 254.

McKenna, Neil, *The Secret Life of Oscar Wilde* (London: Century, 2003).

Medd, Jodie, 'Patterns of the Possible: National Imaginings and Queer Historical (meta)Fictions in Jamie O'Neill's *At Swim, Two Boys*', *GLQ* 13, no. 1 (2006): 31.

Mercier, Vivian, *The Irish Comic Tradition* (Oxford: Oxford University Press, 1962).

Moore, Dermod, *Diary of a Man* (Dublin: Hot Press Books, 2005).

Mulhall, Anne, Wanda Balzano and Moynagh Sullivan, eds., *Irish Post-modernisms and Popular Culture* (Basingstoke: Palgrave Macmillan, 2007)

Ní Chuilleanáin, Eiléan, ed., *The Wilde Legacy* (Dublin: Four Courts Press, 2003).

Norris, Margot, 'A Walk on the Wild(e) Side', in *Quare Joyce*, ed. Joseph Valente (Ann Arbor: University of Michigan Press, 1998), pp. 19–33.

O'Brien, Edna, 'Dramas', *The Paris Review* 110 (1989).

O'Brien, William, *Evening Memories* (London: Maunsel, 1920).

Ó Broin, Leon, *The Prime Informer* (London: Sidgwick & Jackson, 1971).

O'Casey, Sean, *The Freeman's Journal* (15 March 1924), p. 5.

O'Donoghue, Bernard, 'The Journey to Reading Gaol: Sacrifice and Scapegoats in Irish Literature', in *Wilde the Irishman*, ed. Jerusha McCormack (New Haven, Connecticut and London: Yale University Press, 1998).

Ó hAodha, Micheál, *The Importance of Being Micheál: A Portrait of mac Líammóir* (Kerry: Brandon Press, 1990).

O'Neill, Jamie, *At Swim, Two Boys* (London: Scribner, 2001).

O'Sullivan, Michael, *Brendan Behan's Life* (Dublin: Blackwater, 1997).

O'Toole, Fintan, 'Irish Literature in English in the New Millennium', in *The Cambridge History of Irish Literature*, vol. II, 1890–2000, eds. Margaret Kelleher and Philip O'Leary (Cambridge: Cambridge University Press, 2006), pp. 629–41.

Peach, Linden, *The Contemporary Irish Novel* (London: Palgrave, 2004).

Pine, Richard, *Oscar Wilde* (Dublin: Gill & Macmillan, 1983).

—, *The Thief of Reason: Oscar Wilde and Modern Ireland* (Dublin: Gill & Macmillan, 1995).

Pramaggiore, Maria, '"Papa Don't Preach": Pregnancy and Performance in Contemporary Irish Cinema', in *The Irish in US: Irishness, Performativity, and Popular Culture*, ed. Diane Negra (Durham, North Carolina: Duke University Press, 2006), pp. 124–25.

Robinson, Lennox, 'Oscar Wilde', in *I Sometimes Think* (Dublin: Talbot Press, 1956), p. 105.

Roche, Anthony, *The UCD Aesthetic* (Dublin: New Island Books, 2005).

Rose, Kieran, *Diverse Communities: The Evolution of Lesbian and Gay Politics in Ireland* (Cork: Cork University Press, 1994).

Ryan, Patrick, *The Wildes of Merrion Square* (London: Staples Press, 1953).

Sammells, Neil, 'Rediscovering the Wilde Irish', in *Rediscovering Oscar Wilde*, ed. C. George Sandulescu (Gerrards Cross: Colin Smythe, 1994).

Sedgewick, Eve Kosofsky, *Tendencies* (Durham, North Carolina: Duke University Press, 1993).

Sinfield, Alan, '"I See It Is My Name that Terrifies": Wilde in the Twentieth Century', in *The Wilde Legacy*, ed. Eileán Ní Chuilleanáin (Dublin: Four Courts, 2003), pp. 136–52.

—, *Out on Stage* (New Haven, Connecticut: Yale University Press, 1999).

—, Alan, *The Wilde Century: Effeminacy, Oscar Wilde and the Queer Moment* (London: Cassells, 1994).

Sisson, Elaine, *Pearse's Patriots* (Cork: Cork University Press, 2004).

Smyth, Gerry, 'Decolonisation and Criticism: Towards a Theory of Irish Critical Discourse', in *Ireland and Cultural Theory: The Mechanics of Authenticity*, eds. Colin Graham and Richard Kirkland (Basingstoke: Palgrave Macmillan, 1999).

Sturgis, Matthew, *Passionate Attitudes: The English Decadence of the Eighteen Nineties* (London: Macmillan, 1995).

Tóibín, Colm, *Love in a Dark Time: Gay Lives from Wilde to Almodovar* (London: Picador, 2003).

—, *The Master* (London: Picador, 2004).

Toomey, Deirdre, 'Wilde and Orality', in *Wilde the Irishman*, ed. Jerusha McCormack (New Haven, Connecticut and London: Yale University Press, 1998), p. 34.

Valente, Joseph ed., *Quare Joyce* (Ann Arbor: University of Michigan Press, 1998).

Walsh, Fintan, *Queer Notions: New Plays and Performances from Ireland* (Cork: Cork University Press, 2010).

Walshe, Éibhear, 'Wilde's Irish Biographers', *The Wildean* 21 (July 2002): 15-27.

—, ed., *Sex, Nation and Dissent in Irish Writing* (Togher: Cork University Press, 1997).

—, *Kate O'Brien: A Writing Life.* (London: Irish Academic Press, 2006).

— 'Wild(e) Irish'. *Ireland in Proximity.* ed Alderson (London: Routledge, 1999). pp. 64-79.

Weeks, Jeffrey, *Sexuality* (London: Routledge, 2002).

Weintraub, Stanley (ed.), *The Playwright and the Pirate* (Gerrards Cross: Colin Smythe, 1982).

White, Heather, *Wilde Fire* (Fermanagh: Principia Press, 2002).

—, *A Wilde Family* (Fermanagh: Principia Press, 2002).

Wilde, Oscar, *The Collected Letters*, eds. Rupert Hart-Davis and Merlin Holland (London: Fourth Estate, 2000).

—, *The Soul of Man under Socialism* (Oxford: Oxford University Press, 1990).

Wilson, T.G., 'Oscar Wilde at Trinity', *The Practitioner* 173 (October 1954): 473–80.

—, *Victorian Doctor* (London: Methuen, 1942).

Woods, Gregory, *A History of Gay Literature* (New Haven and London: Yale University Press, 1998).

Yeats, W.B., *Autobiographies* (London: Macmillan, 1955).

Index